Jesse Feiler, Gail B. Nayowith
The Nonprofit Risk Book

Jesse Feiler, Gail B. Nayowith

The Nonprofit Risk Book

Finding and Managing Risk in Nonprofits and NGOs

DE
G
PRESS

ISBN 978-1-5015-1516-3
e-ISBN (PDF) 978-1-5015-0594-2
e-ISBN (EPUB) 978-1-5015-0600-0

Library of Congress Cataloging-in-Publication Data
A CIP catalog record for this book has been applied for at the Library of Congress.

Bibliographic information published by the Deutsche Nationalbibliothek
The Deutsche Nationalbibliothek lists this publication in the Deutsche Nationalbibliografie;
detailed bibliographic data are available on the Internet at http://dnb.dnb.de.

© 2017 Jesse Feiler, Gail B. Nayowith
Published by Walter de Gruyter Inc., Boston/Berlin
Printing and binding: CPI books GmbH, Leck
♾ Printed on acid-free paper
Printed in Germany

www.degruyter.com

Acknowledgments

We have been fortunate to have had help and assistance from many people over the years and particularly over the last year in which we have been working on the book and app. Our thanks go out to Jeff Pepper at De Gruyter for putting this book in motion. Jeff has been instrumental in bringing a number of Jesse's books to market, and it is great to be working with him again at De Gruyter. Also on the production side, Carole Jelen at Waterside Productions once again has guided the progress of the book, as have Jaya Dalal and Angie MacAllister's team: they have truly made this book possible.

In addition, Chuck Edwards and his band of beta testers have been helpful in developing the app, while Barbara Butler has also provided insight into important parts of the nonprofit world. Michelle Lawrence in London has helped with international information while Gary Miller and Daniel Starr helped with the New York City cultural scene.

Bill Baccaglini and Jennifer Geiling were early thought partners on risk assessment and why it matters. The Human Services Council pushed our thinking on the sources of nonprofit risk and Gabby Sheely brought fresh insight into the process of enterprise risk planning. Frank and frequent discussions with Larian Angelo about operating risk in local government as contrasted with public universities and other nonprofits, filled an important conceptual gap.

Contents

Introduction

The Nonprofit Risk Book grew out of many years of work in the nonprofit sector in the US and in government-NGO partnerships further from home. In trading stories and adventures over the years, we discovered that many of the biggest challenges affecting nonprofit organizations are very common but rarely discussed. We also learned that many of the toughest issues nonprofits face can be addressed by heeding lessons learned the hard way by others. This book is our attempt to turn experience into useful guidance that can take the sting out of lessons otherwise taught in the school of hard knocks.

Our experience has run the gamut from hyper-local community arts, environment, library and crisis response organizations to multi-jurisdictional civic engagement, advocacy, health and human service organizations and coalitions, with time spent in between, working in and with government and philanthropy. All told, we've each worked for three decades as staff, volunteers, chief executives and board members using our passion for causes and cities in the service of mission-driven organizations and leaders.

We focus on nonprofit and NGO risk because this immediately focuses attention and resources on preventing problems that plague all nonprofits at one time or another. Whether it's a vulnerability caused by an organization's policies or practices or it's a political, economic or environmental threat that comes from the outside, nonprofits and NGOs often find themselves in a tight spot and in need of smart solutions.

About the Book

The book offers a lens through which to think about and manage risk along with a simple toolkit to do so. The idea is to take the guesswork out of risk assessment and mitigation planning so nonprofit executives and boards don't have to learn how to manage risk at the worst possible time—through a critical incident or disastrous circumstance. It is our contention that just like a focus on insuring quality programming and managing performance, enterprise risk management (ERM) is a skill set that should be in every nonprofit leader's repertoire.

Part I: Nonprofit Risk and Mitigation
1. Thinking about Risk
2. Getting Started with Enterprise Risk Management
3. Risk Mitigation Plan Development & Monitoring
4. Making It Work

Part II: Nonprofit Operating Risk
5. Programs & Services
6. Personnel
7. Environment, Regulatory, and Compliance Issues
8. Finance
9. Fundraising
10. Marketing, Communications, and Reputation
11. Operations
12. Technology & Data
13. Board Governance and Oversight

This book has two parts. In the first, we talk about the nature of nonprofit and nongovernmental organizations and speak to the risks all nonprofits face. We offer a simple taxonomy to help orient you to risk and ways to assess vulnerability and risk. We offer a way to prioritize risks and develop mitigation strategies tailored to your organization's unique circumstances. We offer an orientation to the techniques of enterprise risk management. We want to leave executives and boards with a working ability to create an ERM plan and mitigation strategy and build an ERM system that can catch, filter, and address vulnerabilities before they turn into problems in your organization.

The message from the first half of the book includes one universal truth—that risk occurs in *every* nonprofit and risk can emerge in *any* nonprofit activity—and ten takeaways:
1. Risk can be exacerbated or abated by organizational policies, practices, processes, people and technology platforms.

2. Sometimes a risk is so flagrant and obvious it is shocking that it has gone unnoticed, and because it hasn't been dealt with, the risk has created dysfunction that has bled into every aspect of the organization's programs and operations.

3. There is an interaction effect between risk and poor management where sleepy management, fuzzy management roles and a shaky decision-making hierarchy is the root cause of serious organizational risk.

4. There is an interaction linking risk and governance where sleepy governance, inconsistent oversight, role confusion and/or troubled communication is at the root of risk in the organization.

5. Weak business process, lack of formalized policies, limited training and inconsistent supervision to reinforce good practice often interact to create risk.

6. Risk management enhances, and is no substitute for, strategic planning, corporate compliance, quality assurance or performance management activities in an organization.

7. Organization size and complexity factor into an organization's ability to withstand serious risks.

8. Reliance on poorly paid staff and volunteers is a special challenge for nonprofit organizations.

9. The nonprofit business model and reliance on government contracts and fundraising revenue breeds risk.

10. Nonprofit risk, while akin to commercial business risk, has unique features that require tailored risk identification strategies and specialized mitigation solutions.

Looking at risk from different perspectives rather than from one view point can help you understand and be comfortable with the complexity you are looking at. In Part I, we show you several perspectives to help you think flexibly about the project you are undertaking.

In the second part of the book, we delve into the functional areas of nonprofit operations from programs and personnel to fundraising and governance. These chapters cover risk, risk clusters and risk interactions in key areas of nonprofit operations that, left unattended, can interrupt services or seriously derail operations and your attention to mission.

We don't write about specific organizations or individuals—this is not a book of case studies—but about risk and vulnerabilities as recurring themes that we have observed time and again in our own work. While examples touch on all areas of nonprofit risk, we don't limit discussion to topics covered elsewhere by colleagues in the insurance, audit, finance or legal services businesses. Our examples come from lived experience and are intended to prime your thinking, prompt action and make you shake your head. Our slant offers a window into some hard to believe and some not-at-all hard to believe nonprofit risks. The idea is that before dismissing any of the risk situations presented as something that cannot happen in your organization, we want you to stop and think about some of the mundane and outlandish things that come across your desk every day, those that you deal with routinely as a matter of course, and imagine what would happen if you hadn't dealt with them.

In addition to authoring this book, we now approach the issues of nonprofit risk in our consulting work and in The Nonprofit Risk App, a new tool we developed to make risk identification and risk management easier. It is available for iPhone and iPad in the App Store at http://apple.co/2fUXZqw. You can also use the downloadable PDF forms we have posted on our website at champlainarts.com/nprisk.

We encourage you to make space in your organization for risk assessment and management using whatever tools will work best for yourself and your organization: this book, the app, the literature on nonprofit risk, and/or an engagement with a consultant or firm. We conclude by cheering on all efforts to locate and address risk in nonprofit organizations that matter to you.

Notwithstanding all the help and assistance we have received from so many people, any errors are ours.

Feel free to contact us at nprisk@champlainarts.com.

Part I: **Nonprofit Risk and Mitigation**

Chapter 1
Thinking About Risk

We began talking about risk after reading report after report of high-profile business failures in well-regarded nonprofit organizations. The tragic downfall of these organizations, long known for providing important and even essential services, left us wondering why nonprofits and NGOs go belly-up and whether there was something to be done that could prevent or change this outcome. From these conversations and our experience leading, working as staff and volunteers, and serving on boards, *The Nonprofit Risk Book* was born.

As we began scanning the field in search of clues, patterns and examples emerged with alarming clarity. We found countless instances of nonprofit organizations, large and small, that had failed to heed warning signs or assumed they were too small, too large or too well-run to be harmed by risks common to nonprofits and NGOs. This point is well illustrated by the collapse of Hull House, FEGS, New York City Opera and Kids Company. Jane Addams established Hull House in a poor immigrant Chicago neighborhood in 1889 (built on ideas taken from Toynbee Hall, a settlement house that opened in London's East End five years earlier). The Jane Addams Hull House Association became a pillar of the community and a fixture in the national social welfare scene. On January 19, 2012, Hull House unexpectedly announced bankruptcy and their anticipated closure. Within a week, employees were told that there would be no severance pay, no health insurance coverage, and no accrued vacation pay. The community residents served by Hull House were told they'd have to go elsewhere for assistance. The impact of the closure shocked not only employees and people served by Hull House, but it also left a gap in the city's safety net, causing strain and worry across the city. How could such a respected and storied organization close suddenly after 122 years?

Just like Hull House and also seemingly without warning in 2015, FEGS Health and Human Services notified New York State and City governments that it had a $20 million deficit and would be closing its doors after 80 years of operation. These calls sent New York City and State leaders scrambling almost overnight to find sponsors for $250 million in programs serving 100,000 people, and jobs for a workforce of over 4,000 employees. As the story unwound, it became clear that early warning signs were missed or ignored.

It's not just in social welfare and human services that these cataclysmic nonprofit failures have occurred. The New York City Opera was founded in 1943 with the goal of making opera accessible to a wide audience and, as years went on, with a secondary goal of supporting new American singers and composers. It became a part of Lincoln Center for the Performing Arts in 1966 and found a home at the New York State Theater at Lincoln Center where it performed for 45 years. Financial difficulties caused it to move from its performance home at Lincoln Center in 2011 to office space

DOI 10.1515/9781501505942-001

elsewhere in Manhattan. A few operas were performed at other venues in New York City, but on October 1, 2013, the New York City Opera filed for bankruptcy after a 70-year run. As of this writing, the New York City Opera is operating on a much smaller scale in a new format at other locations. While the story is not finished, the Opera's future is not secure.

Problems like this are not limited to the United States or to long-established organizations. Kids Company was founded in 1996 to serve vulnerable children in London and, later, in Liverpool and Bristol. It grew rapidly, and by 2013 had a budget of £23 million and a staff of nearly 500 employees. Starting in 2009, various warning signs began to appear. By August 5, 2015, the charity closed its doors.

These organizations and others that have suffered the same fate offer important lessons. The rate of nonprofit closures has accelerated at an unprecedented pace, raising alarms for boards and executive leadership, as well as foundations, donors, governments, and the public. Each nonprofit failure, whether from insolvency or poor management, raises serious questions about the integrity and functioning of all nonprofits.

When a nonprofit or NGO fails, two questions are usually asked: "How did it happen?" and "Can it happen to us?" This kind of forensic or post-action review typically provides a case study in poor management, limited oversight, and little else. Rarely does a nonprofit's collapse generate lessons that forward-thinking leaders can use to make their own organizations work better or protect them from the same fate.

Often, nonprofit leaders look at these organizational failures and see no immediate cause for alarm or action on their part. They see an extreme set of conditions and circumstances that don't seem to apply to their organizations. Smart leaders know that there is more to the story.

The fact is that in each of these cases, there were warning signs that went unheeded. Before the crisis that led to closure, there were incidents that, in retrospect, should have been seen as critical moments where changes could have been made to avert the disasters. Even where major problems occurred, in retrospect critical inflection points stand out where mitigation efforts could have lessened the blow.

This book helps you identify risks before they present themselves as calamities. It applies to leaders of small and large organizations, multiple location and single program operations and organizations that rely on paid staff or are 100% volunteer led because risk is endemic. In other words, risk management applies to everyone who has management or governance responsibility for a nonprofit organization. So we begin with the basics—identifying risk. Without identifying risks, there is no way to mitigate them, so this book starts with the process of identifying risks. Then, with risks identified, we help you plan your mitigation actions. From identified risks and planned mitigation actions, we move to active implementation, tracking and oversight while keeping an eye on any emerging risks to be certain that they are controlled.

What's Special About Nonprofit Risk?

Nonprofit organizations operate in a complex environment characterized by risk, but many nonprofit leaders have limited experience engaging risk actively. Nonprofit executives manage to mission. They believe that if they are doing good, only good things will happen. They rely on a cherished belief that a mission focus will protect them. While it's true that a mission focus—*doing good*—is the distinguishing feature of nonprofit organizations, when all attention and resources are focused on activities that serve constituents or causes, organizations can lose sight of their underlying business operations and operating environments, making them more prone to risks that could have been identified and mitigated earlier. This blind spot is where nonprofit risk management begins. It is also at the heart of what distinguishes the practice of risk management in the nonprofit and commercial worlds.

Risk creates organizational distress that causes nonprofits and NGOs to lose their ability to make wise choices. Time, talent, attention, and resources shift to crisis mode and all other organizational activities take a back seat to addressing this urgent, immediate need. Managing crises is costly—astronomical amounts of money are spent directly on injuries, damages and settlements, lawyers and reputation management, and indirectly on staff time diverted to addressing and cleaning up the fallout.

The disruptions caused by nonprofit failures have moved the discussion of risk from an "it-can't-happen-here" mentality and from the purview of accounting firms, auditors, the insurance industry, and charity watchdogs who are typically the custodians of organizational risk, to the nonprofit boardroom and executive suite. The following sections offer a framework for thinking about nonprofit risk, along with an overview of typical risks affecting nonprofit organizations and how to uncover and deal with them. In the chapters of Part II, you'll find details on how to bring enterprise risk management into your organization and how to find and manage risk.

The Nonprofit Business Model Creates Risks for Many Nonprofit Organizations

The nonprofit business model presents a unique environment for risk. There are six challenges that are carried by most nonprofits as a matter of course. These risks are viewed as the price of doing business in the nonprofit sector and they are vastly different from risks carried by commercial enterprises.

- *Multi-year government contracts* with flat funding can cause budget deficits because the cost of providing services increases every year but contract funding does not.

- *Complex program eligibility* can make it hard to identify people who are approved to attend a program or use a service. This can leave the organization with programs that are not fully subscribed, or, on the other hand, ineligible participants who receive services for which there is no reimbursement from funders.
- *Required fundraising matches* to cover basic operating expenses for services otherwise supported by a government contract or need to increase fees beyond what patrons or recipients can afford in order to generate sufficient operating revenue.
- *Increasing costs of doing business* with no steady source of additional revenue to cover staff salaries and benefits, supplies and materials, and costs that grow each year.
- *Growing demand* that exceeds the organization's ability to respond, creating long waiting lists, poor client relationship management, and community dissatisfaction.
- *Rigorous performance requirements* and the need for back-office operations that require new technology, a data analytics team, or quality improvement activities that are not reimbursed through government contracts or through private fundraising which favors direct support to programs and services.

These and other nonprofit risks are discussed generally in Part I and in more detail as essential nonprofit functions in Part II.

6 Common Warning Signs of Underlying Risk

The challenges outlined in the previous section are the operating reality for most nonprofit organizations large or small. The six warning signs outlined in this section are proxies for underlying risk. Where these problems occur, risk is sure to follow.

- *No regularly scheduled budget oversight* or *monitoring.* This means no controls on spending or recognition of deficits and a serious lapse in board governance.
- *Limited data sharing on agency activities, operations, or performance, and no routinely scheduled incident, program, and back-office performance review.* This means the organization is not learning from experience or correcting mistakes.
- *Limited communication, irregular feedback, or no corrective action monitoring.* This means there is little shared understanding of or accountability for achieving goals.
- *Late filings or late submissions of required tax, financial, grant, or government reports.* This puts the organization in jeopardy of penalties, revocation of charity status or non-renewal of essential government or foundation grants.
- *High staff turnover or low productivity.* This red flag suggests a troubled work environment and the provision of low-quality services.

- *Poor client relationship management and customer service.* This means that service recipients do not get what they need and often leave early before completing the program.

If one or more of these risks exist in your organization, you should prepare to dig deeper to identify the cause and act on them as quickly as possible using mitigation strategies you will find in Chapter 3.

What Is Risk?

Risk identification, management, prevention, and control have become more important across all types of organizations. The previous sections focused on some specific nonprofit concerns, but this section covers a broader spectrum of risks that affect all business operations. They are the basics when it comes to contemporary risk discussions. The descriptions of risk in this section can help orient you to the concept of risk and get everyone in your organization speaking the same language about risk. Understanding risk is the first step in being able to work together to identify, mitigate, and manage your organization's risk.

The classic definitions of risk focus on misfortunes that may occur. To be more specific, risk is often defined as the potential to gain or lose something of value. In a business context, risk is described as the probability, threat, susceptibility, or consequence of damage, injury, hazard, liability, loss, or any other negative event, situation, or condition caused by internal or external vulnerabilities that may be avoided through prospective or preemptive action.

For nonprofits and NGOs, risk can be regarded as any issue that may cause an organization to lose sight of or divert from its mission, purpose, or daily operations. Risk can come from a single event or from multiple vulnerabilities interacting across some or all of an organization's departments, divisions, or functions.

Traditionally, organizations consider financial risks such as fraud and cash management practices, whether it spends too much on fundraising, or if it relies on a few large donors. But *non-financial* risk creates as much vulnerability for nonprofits and NGOs as it does for commercial businesses. After the global financial crisis of 2008, and the corporate governance and ethics problems that have emerged over the last several decades, more attention is being paid to risk in all of its forms across all types of organizations. Most contemporary definitions of risk go beyond misfortunes that may actually occur to risk scenario planning that includes the possible effects of uncertainty on organizational goals.

Individual risks can be characterized in many ways, but there are three sets of descriptors that apply to all risks:
- *Types of risk.* Describes the sort and scope of risk.
- *Dimensions of risk.* Describes the source of risk and the degree of harm caused by risk.
- *Categories of risk.* Describes risks in the context of key organizational functions.

Identifying and describing the particular set of risks facing your organization is an important element in enterprise risk management. The clearer risks are defined in your organization, the better. The following sections of *The Nonprofit Risk Book* include ways to describe risks in greater detail.

Types of Risk

Risks can be *episodic* and *incident-driven* with one outsized situation or problem causing harm to your organization. Risks can also be *systemic* or *structural*. These risks are those that appear regularly and are generated by something baked into an organization's operations (usually as a byproduct of other initiatives or ways of working). Risk can occur through a complex chain of events or clustering of problems that interact and magnify the significance of individual factors to cause harm to your organization.

Dimensions of Risk

Thanks to work being done on corporate compliance and enterprise risk management in the for-profit and not-for-profit sector by organizations like The Committee of Sponsoring Organizations of the Treadway Commission (COSO), International Organization for Standardization (ISO), Chartered Global Management Accountants (CGMA), BDO USA and Deloitte US, nonprofit and NGO leaders are learning to think about the specific features of risk and the degree of harm that can result from risks left unaddressed. We call this the *dimensions of risk*. Understanding the dimensions of risk will help you look for, identify, prioritize, and begin to manage risk. There are four basic dimensions of risk: source, likelihood, impact, and vulnerability.
- *Source.* Does the threat or concern originate from inside or outside of my organization?
- *Likelihood.* What is the probability that this risk has, can, or will occur in my organization? Is this risk very likely, moderately likely, or not very likely to occur?
- *Impact.* How significant will the effect of this risk be on my organization? How serious could the consequences of this risk be for my organization? Is this a high risk, medium risk, or low risk?
- *Vulnerability.* Is my organization safe from this risk? How much risk exposure does my organization have?

Categories of Risk

All nonprofits and NGOs will find risk across all functional areas, departments, divisions, and programs. By thinking holistically and looking functionally, you can help each member of your team locate risks that are central to their everyday work and portfolio of responsibilities. There is a series of questions you can pose to your team that can help them focus on specific risks in your organization. These general questions will help you drill down to the processes and practices that may pose specific risks for your organization. Risk in each functional area of operations is discussed more fully in its own chapter.

5 Operating Risks in Key Organizational Pillars

The functional areas of an organization—its departments, divisions, and programs— are home to operating risks. Operating risk comes from a breakdown, misalignment, misuse, or misunderstanding of goals, tools, or processes. We consider five organizational pillars in which risk presents itself:

- *People.* The people you serve, as well as the people who work inside your organization. Their wants, needs, skills, education, motivations, and goals all come into play in the daily operations of your organization.
- *Policy.* These are the formal rules that you set or are set for you, as well as the informal guidelines that may be handed down from founders or other leaders of the organization, that govern the daily operations of your organization.
- *Practice.* This is how things are actually done. Practice is what people do and how they do it. It can reflect formal or informal customs, conventions, culture, or habit.
- *Process.* The ways in which things are done. This describes workflow and a set of formalized activities or repeatable steps to reach organizational goals.
- *Technology.* In today's world of work, technology is everywhere and part of everything we do. It is the hardware and software that processes information and facilitates communication. It can be used fully, partially, or worked around.

Why Nonprofit Enterprise Risk Management Matters

Risk lives in every organization and aspect of organizational operations. But the risk mix, likelihood of occurrence, and potential impact differ from organization to organization, necessitating a careful look by department, program, and function to identify vulnerabilities. Enterprise risk management (ERM) is the discipline that looks at organizational risk and searches for patterns and combinations that need a broad approach to identification and mitigation.

Enterprise risk management can shield your organization from internal vulnerabilities and external threats, giving you breathing room to respond to new opportunities. Most nonprofits and NGO leaders are so busy dealing with day-to-day activities that they find themselves stretched to keep up. They experience the thought of adding one more thing to the to-do list to be overwhelming and they believe that managing to mission will protect them from disaster. These leaders don't realize that:

- Disjointed one-off crisis response drains energy and resources.
- The fear of identifying risks doesn't mean they won't happen.
- Risks can be mitigated by baking solutions into daily operations.
- Denial, "it-can't-happen-here," or "it's-out-of-our-control" ways of thinking are surefire breeding grounds for risk.
- There are ways to identify resources, capture data, and develop indicators to monitor and respond to emerging risk events.

Once leaders consider the disruption, expense, and effort it takes to manage a crisis and imagine the peace of mind that can come when problems are averted or mitigated, the work of enterprise risk management becomes more appealing.

As leaders move into the work of risk management, they must consider the aggregate amount of risk the organization actually carries and bears—its *risk profile*—and its ability to tolerate and balance risk-taking—*the risk appetite*:

- *Risk profile* is the overall level of risk in which your organization operates.
- *Appetite for risk* is the amount of risk an organization is willing to take to reach its goals and how risk-averse or daring the organization is.

Risk Profile

Understanding the aggregate amount of risk associated with organizational performance and operations is the first step in a process to mitigate it. Organizational risk is assessed along a continuum, as there is no universal risk profile for all nonprofits or NGOs.

An organization's risk profile is based upon an assessment of internal weaknesses, external threats, and leadership's ability to tolerate exposure and vulnerabilities. The risk profile you develop will take your mission, strategy, plans, and objectives and marry it with executive and board tolerance for uncertainty and surprise. The risk profile will consider known, new, or emerging risks, and it will contemplate three additional types of risk: *preventable risk* that is usually related to internal practices that can be improved, *strategy risk* that contemplates likely risks and plans to contain them, and *external risk* that cannot be controlled but can be anticipated and mitigated with advance preparation.

Assessing an organization's risk profile is not about compliance and audits, nor is it about rules and regulations. Checklists and rules-based risk models do not diminish the likelihood or impact of risk events or the impact of cascading risk. Understanding your risk profile will enable you to anchor risk assessment to risk mitigation activities throughout your organization.

As with many challenges in life, actively managing risk means knowing and accepting your own strengths and limitations. To deal with risk, you must know how much of it your organization, staff, and leadership can bear and come to the work with an understanding of your organization's capacity to manage it. The process of developing your risk profile starts by figuring out your appetite for risk.

Appetite for Risk

The organization needs to determine how much risk it is willing to accept in pursuing its goals. This can change over time. Determining appetite is an exercise in finding the sweet spot between risk and opportunity. The appetite for risk is usually measured as a vulnerability parameter in one or more functional areas of operations: financial, operational, programmatic, and strategic.

Every organization faces different risks, so a one-size-fits-all risk management program is not possible. The experience and knowledge of volunteers, board members and staff should be the basis for developing a sound risk management program. Risk management is the thoughtful process of recognizing and controlling risks so you can protect and conserve resources. Your risk management program should cover all aspects of your organization, including its mission, services, strategic goals, activities, staffing, funding, and ongoing operations. It is far better to plan for risk than to deal with problems, so it is important for the organization to have a sense of the amount and types of risk it can handle comfortably.

Summary

This chapter provides an overview and general description of risk in the nonprofit world. The following chapter will guide you through identifying specific risks in your organization.

Chapter 2
Getting Started with Enterprise Risk Management

One reason we wrote *The Nonprofit Risk Book* is to take the guesswork out of what should be standard management practice within all nonprofits and NGOs. Once we started untangling the lessons learned from high profile nonprofit closures, we concluded that what seemed like a basic management tool was absent too often to be a simple oversight. We returned again and again to the operating reality of most nonprofits and NGOs—that leaders throughout the sector have their hands and plates full. There is seemingly no time in these lean organizations to hunt down hidden problems... until a crisis or tragedy strikes. The idea of this book is to help you build a risk management program and toolkit that prevents you from having to learn lessons the hard way.

This chapter begins with a focused examination of Enterprise Risk Management (ERM) and goes deeper into the discussion of nonprofit risk assessment and how to locate and understand specific risks in your organization. At the end of this chapter, you will be able to identify risks in your organization and complete a risk assessment using a paper or online app template. These activities will contribute to the development of an ERM plan using tools discussed later in Chapter 3.

Defining Enterprise Risk Management

Broadly speaking, risk is the possibility of something bad happening. When it comes to risk, we try our best to avoid it whenever possible. When we can't avoid it, we try to manage it—like carrying an umbrella on days when rain is predicted. Risk avoidance and management is something we learn to do as individuals, but it also is something nonprofit leaders do for their organizations. A holistic approach to risk management across all organization operations is called *enterprise risk management* (ERM).

Enterprise risk management isn't just about risk. ERM improves decision-making and day-to-day operations. It's also about performance and strategy. It enhances an organization's effectiveness by linking mission to action. In pursuing its mission, every nonprofit or NGO operates in an environment of uncertainty where things are never completely known. Enterprise risk management allows an organization to balance uncertainty and exposure. Enterprise risk management planning will help you answer several important questions, such as:

- What is our organization's appetite for risk?
- How much risk can our organization handle?
- What is the best way for us to reduce risk?
- Do we have the right people to handle risk?
- How will we know that we've eliminated or reduced the potential impact of a risk event or a cluster of risk events?

DOI 10.1515/9781501505942-002

Nonprofit Enterprise Risk Management Defined

Enterprise risk management for nonprofits and NGOs is defined as an approach that enables an organization to reach its strategic goals by reducing uncertainty, vulnerability, and exposure to events and activities that divert attention and resources away from its purpose and mission.

Getting Started with Enterprise Risk Management

Recognizing and managing risk is different than managing strategy. Thinking about risk centers on negative threats and failures versus a strategic focus on opportunities and successes. It is a counterintuitive mental model for most nonprofit leaders. In general, risk is hard to discuss because people tend to overestimate their ability to control life events that are actually controlled by chance. Behavioral scientists have found that people are inclined to be overconfident about their ability to predict risk, yet lack the ability to predict the full range of outcomes that can occur. There is a tendency to extrapolate from recent experience and apply this understanding and perception to an uncertain future. This confirmation bias drives us to favor information that supports our position and to discount information that challenges or contradicts this viewpoint. It becomes even more challenging when an event diverges from expectations, because most people escalate and cling tighter to their views and commitments.

These biases play out in an organization's inability to talk about and explore mistakes and failures *without* judgment. The uncertainty with which most nonprofits operate and the human inclination to confirmation bias explains why leaders and organizations often overlook, discount, and delay action on emerging risks. Early warnings often come as ambiguous smoke signals and symptoms that suggest that something is amiss. Early warnings investigated and resolved differentiate false alarms from critical alerts.

Enterprise risk management is a disciplined way of dealing with uncertainty and threats. It creates an awareness that helps organizations identify and control risks. As a way of thinking and acting, risk management requires cultural and organizational discipline in the form of management processes and policies. By codifying performance expectations in rules and preferred actions, an organization's policies and business processes enable staff to cope with uncertainty. By strengthening business processes and policies, leaders are able to prevent lapses, promote quality and protect vital resources. ERM provides a framework for identifying risks and deciding what to do about them and in what priority. Because risk is ever present in all nonprofits and NGOs, risk identification, assessment, and mitigation planning should be integrated into all aspects of organization activity.

A guiding framework for recognizing and acting on risks might look like this:

Step 1. Look for risks by asking what could go wrong in the future and what has gone wrong in the past in the organization and in similar organizations. In what ways is the organization vulnerable to risk? Could these risks recur?

Step 2. Consider the ways risks could affect the organization and where these risks would hit hardest within the organization. Use scenarios to stress test operations. What risks should be prioritized and handled first?

Step 3. Consider ways to control risk and risk reducing mitigation actions that could be taken. What are we prepared to do or change in order to reduce risk? What capacity and resources can be deployed to address risk?

Step 4. How will we knit together our risk mitigation efforts to make an ERM program and plan? How will we integrate ERM activities into our other quality improvement and performance management activities? Who should be involved in developing and implementing solutions?

Teeing Up the ERM Planning Process

There are three stages of any ERM planning process: Readiness and Rollout, Risk Identification and Assessment, and Risk Mitigation Plan Development and Monitoring. We describe these three distinct stages in Figure. 2.1, which flows sequentially to make the process easy to follow. In practice, the stages can overlap.

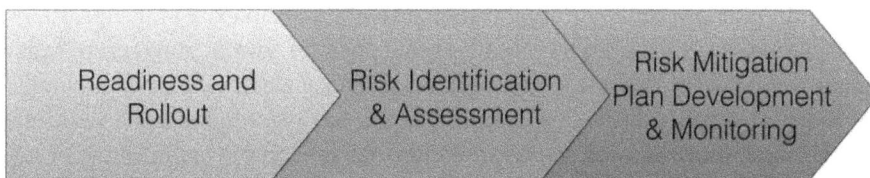

Figure 2.1: ERM Process Overview

Let's take the stages one by one.

- *Readiness and rollout.* This is the process of raising awareness, getting ready, and rolling out ERM. Getting staff and board members to focus may be the most difficult part of the process. This book offers useful guidance to motivate people and help you work through organizational resistance.
- *Risk identification and assessment.* This is the process of identifying and analyzing risks that can harm your organization. This book helps you identify areas of vulnerability and risk within your organization and in the external operating environment. It also offers a framework to help you decide which risks are most important and how to prioritize them.
- *Risk mitigation plan development and monitoring.* This is the process of combining your priority risks with planned actions to resolve them and building a protocol to monitor progress. This book offers templates to help you determine your organization's risks, establish priorities, and design a risk mitigation plan.

Along with the staging of the ERM planning process, there are also important considerations about who will lead the process and how long it will take. Setting up an ERM planning process for the first time can be challenging. Some nonprofit organizations choose to manage the ERM planning process with existing staff. Others prefer to bring in a consultant to organize and facilitate the process. In either case, naming a project manager is essential. Ideally, the project manager is a well-respected staff member who knows the organization and is known for getting things done. Whenever possible, establishing an ERM Planning Team to work hand-in-hand with the Project Manager is desirable. Project planning software that links activities and deadlines can help organize the work and work assignments.

Another consideration in the ERM process is the amount of time it will take to complete and implement the ERM plan. The biggest factor in estimating the timeline for an ERM project is the organization's size and complexity of its operations. A small organization staffed by volunteers that operates several programs or runs a single annual event like one concert and a half-dozen classroom music programs, sponsors a workshop for young composers, and has two fundraisers a year, may need a longer timeframe to complete the ERM than a nonprofit organization of similar size staffed by paid employees. Similarly, a large multi-service, multi-site organization that relies on a mix of paid staff and volunteers may need several months to complete its ERM plan.

You should expect each stage of the ERM planning process to take several full days (up to 21 hours) that are spread out over the course of a 6–12-week period. Some experts believe you can do a rudimentary ERM plan in one full day session. What matters most is that you give yourself and your team clear direction on the task and enough time away from daily activities to observe and reflect. You should plan to build in a minimum of one meeting at each stage for discussion about findings and to make decisions about future actions and next steps.

Stage 1. Readiness and Rollout

All ERM programs start with a frank assessment of organization structure, culture, and capabilities. An organization's culture is expressed through its activities and performance. It is expressed in what staff, managers, and leaders say and do, how they do it, and what they strive to do. Organization capabilities are the unique combination of talent and resources available to deliver on an organization's mission. How the organization delivers its services and organizes itself to get its work done will shape the ERM process.

Smart leaders know that complacency is the enemy of organizational effectiveness. They know that it corrodes culture, alienates clients and staff, and stifles curiosity. For ERM to work, leaders need to value problem solving and build a culture that values learning and testing new ways to solve old problems.

Smart leaders can forecast opportunities on the horizon and the possibility of something going wrong. They know that some risks are worth taking, while others could prove disastrous for their organization. They know that there is no way to avoid risk and they understand that taking risks is vital for impact. An effective ERM process requires leaders to know their own appetite for risk and the risk tolerance limits of their boards and organization.

Step 1. Taking Stock of Your Organization and Its Readiness for ERM

As you begin thinking about introducing ERM to your organization, you will want to take stock of your organization's readiness to engage in this kind of focused effort (Figure. 2.2). It helps to think through questions that will allow you to gauge how open or prepared your board and staff members are for a deep dive into the mechanics of your organization's operations. Start by thinking about your organization's legal structure and its life cycle, culture, and experience with planning. Here are some questions to consider: Are we a start-up or legacy organization or something in-between? Do we have an annual goals document developed with board, department, and program managers and staff? Have we implemented a strategic or business plan successfully before? Are board and staff comfortable working across departments, programs, and divisions? Are we an internally-facing organization making management hires and promotions from within? Are staff members comfortable with accountability and performance expectations? Are we comfortable talking about risk and mistakes? How receptive is our organization to change?

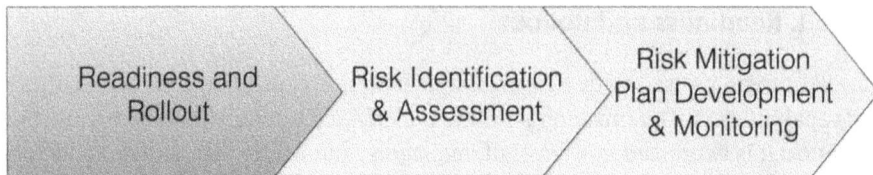

Figure 2.2: Readiness and rollout

Here are some additional questions to consider at the beginning of your ERM planning process.

– *Organization structure.* How is your organization structured? Are you an association, network, or federation? Do you have subsidiaries? Do you have a single administrative entity and one set of policies, or are affiliates managing their own back office and setting their own policies? Are your activities housed in one office or are your operations spread out across locations? Are liabilities shared by the organization or held by affiliates?

– *Governance structure.* How does your board of directors operate? Are roles and responsibilities formalized and are bylaws up to date? Are terms of office specified or open? Do you operate with active board committees or an executive committee?

– *Management structure.* How does the organization operate? Do you have a strong executive or a management team approach? Is your management hierarchy—reporting lines, span of control, roles and responsibilities, and decision-making authority—clearly delineated or fluid? Do staff and volunteers know what their responsibilities are and to whom they report?

– *Business model.* What services do you provide and how do you deliver and pay for them? Do you provide a single service or are you a multi-service organization? Do you hold government contracts or receive government funding? Are you privately funded for all or part of your work? Do you monitor program quality or performance? Are you staffed by employees, volunteers, or independent contractors? Do you operate in a single or across multiple jurisdictions?

Why Do a Readiness Assessment?

Investing time and resources in risk signals a shift in perspective at the top of the organization. Preparing for ERM planning begins the critical process of heightening the risk awareness of board, managers, staff, and volunteers, as well as your funders, government partners, and vendors. Getting ready to do ERM planning will expose areas of vulnerability and raise staff anxiety. This will surface resistance in departments and programs that are not running as well as they could, and will generate enthusiasm in departments and programs where quality and performance improvement is highly valued. ERM establishes an expectation that the organization will begin look-ing for and assessing risk through focused attention and a deliberate process. It puts everyone on notice that identified risks and areas of vulnerability will be actively managed and that risks identified will be mitigated. Setting the tone at the top is key to moving forward with an organization-wide process of reflection and self-assess-ment around risk.

ERM readiness preparation begins with a series of questions: What are our big-gest vulnerabilities and where are we most vulnerable to threats? What could possi-bly go wrong and how would it affect the organization? What can we do to prevent risk and what actions will we take if something bad happens?

Is the Organization Prepared to Change?

The arc of change begins with a focus on enterprise risk management and ends with new levels of accountability and improved monitoring, reporting and performance. For nonprofits and NGOs with sophisticated performance management, continuous quality improvement, or compliance processes, adding a focus on risk will feel like a continuation of work already underway. For organizations that come to ERM by way of a financial crisis, lawsuit, critical incident, or other crisis, or whose knowledge about day-to-day operations is communicated anecdotally or informally, the level of scrutiny and responsibility generated by a focused assessment of risk may be unwel-come or resisted. In either case, the change initiated by the ERM process will need to be supported and actively managed.

You'll know that you've hit a pocket of resistance when discussion of risk is met with responses that include verbal or behavioral pushback:

"We don't need this."

"We know where our risks are."

"We don't want to substitute creativity and mission focus for a focus on compli-ance."

"We tried this before and it didn't work."

"We already do this."

"We're overworked and cannot take on additional responsibilities."

The starting point for ERM, like any organizational change, is to identify a hand-ful of people who have an affinity for innovation and improvement and who instinc-tively look for opportunities to stretch and grow the impact of their work. A small band of ERM enthusiasts can help you prepare to bring the organization along.

When ERM is working in an organization, everyone is on the same page and feels the same level of urgency to identify, follow up and cure outstanding issues. In or-ganizations with a robust ERM focus, there are quarterly meetings of a Board Risk or Quality Improvement Committee in addition to monthly staff-level meetings to review progress made in addressing identified risks. The board and staff greet these meetings as an opportunity to strengthen operations and practices and to improve quality and performance. When ERM is integrated seamlessly into agency operations, its full value becomes apparent.

Step 2. Find Champions and Build a Team

Thinking about your organization as the sum of its parts helps everyone take responsibility for identifying and managing risk. Engaging program, department, and division heads, managers, supervisors, front-line staff, volunteers, and boards in thinking about risk increases the likelihood that issues will be identified early. The earlier a problem is identified, the greater the chances are of resolving it before it turns into a crisis or does damage. It allows many eyes and ears to look and listen for things that could harm your organization and affect its ability to achieve its goals or do high-quality work.

The idea behind ERM is to take a comprehensive look at risk within departments, job functions, and across the entire organization. Within each functional area of operation—whether it be a program or line of business, finance, back-office administration or support —your team can assess vulnerabilities related to their job duties or areas of responsibility. You will want to establish a solution-oriented and non-judgmental environment to encourage your project manager or team to share information, be forthcoming about mistakes made, acknowledge weaknesses, and propose solutions to risks identified in their operation.

Step 3. Engage Managers, Staff, and Board in Risk Assessment

Talking about risk and how to avoid it is an essential part of enterprise risk management. Educating board officers, managers, employees, and volunteers about risk will help prevent mistakes caused by ignorance and will ground all activities in an awareness and understanding of organizational culture and ways of working. People must fully understand what they need to do, how they may do it, and what they cannot do.

Just like a focus on program quality or performance, it is important to make conversations about risk and risk awareness an everyday activity. Setting the tone at the top and reinforcing risk awareness through training, supervision, annual staff performance reviews, and in standing meetings creates a climate where managers and staff can actively engage in risk identification and assessment activities and provide regular updates as the process unfolds.

Here are four ways to communicate your commitment to better manage risk and your intention to engage all board, staff, interns, and volunteers in risk awareness and enterprise risk management activities.

Introduce the concepts of risk and risk management when you onboard new employees, interns, volunteers, and board members. Hold an orientation and provide a description of the organization's approach to risk management in handbooks for new employees, board members, interns, and volunteers. The orientation will have a broader focus but it should include a discussion of performance, a definition of risk, and description of risk management activities.

Build a risk management focus into training and supervision. Provide training, annual refreshers, and regular supervision for staff, interns, and volunteers so they learn the organization's goals, values, expectations, and desired practices. Include a discussion of risk and how to handle it as an ongoing conversation in each session.

Include risk management discussion items on standing meeting agendas. Incorporate a discussion of risk and risk management into regularly scheduled monthly or quarterly meetings with staff to help them identify risk in their areas of responsibility, discuss how risk is handled now, and create a plan for how to more effectively manage and mitigate risk.

Establish a risk committee or vest a standing committee with responsibility for monitoring risk. Include a discussion of risk and risk management at board meetings and task one board committee with responsibility for monitoring implementation of ERM plan activities. Help the board understand the organization's risks and risk profile. Accept that like quality improvement and performance management, risk identification will be ongoing and that engaging in active governance around risk mitigation activities is important.

When beginning an ERM planning process, it is important to know that the board and senior management team are ready to commit the time needed to construct and implement the plan. Whether staff led or consultant facilitated, the board, project manager or team selected to lead the ERM effort must set the tone at the top and insure that the necessary risk mitigations activities outlined in your ERM plan (policies, processes, and practices) are implemented. Your organization will be well served if you convene a work group of managers, staff, and volunteers to help inform the project manager or team during ERM plan development. The configuration of team members will depend on what makes sense for your organization. It's important to constitute an ERM planning team that spans program, administrative, financial, and back-office functions. What's key is putting together an enthusiastic and engaged ERM team and doing the necessary preparation to communicate ERM to managers and line staff.

It's important to consider the readiness and receptivity of staff and volunteers to the ERM process and devise a plan to address concerns, resistance, and apathy. This can be done in a kick-off meeting and through smaller department or program discussions. You can use the time to inform, educate, and raise awareness of organizational risk, why mitigation is necessary, and why ERM is everyone's concern and responsibility.

Step 4. Frame out the Process

This book includes templates to simplify the risk assessment and mitigation plan development process. The templates are available in a paper or app format. Using these templates as guides will allow you to jump-start your ERM planning and create a first-generation plan. Over time, your team can customize or adapt the framework to meet your needs.

The templates and other guides in *The Nonprofit Risk Book* will help you focus your time and resources on creating an ERM plan in real time. The plan itself can be developed over a period of weeks, depending on the size of the organization and capacity of the ERM project manager or team. Implementation and monitoring activities will typically roll out over a 6 to 9-month period and run between 12 to 18 months, depending on the plan scope and the infrastructure in place. Start the process by creating a description of the ERM process, it's goals and a timeline for your ERM planning process and share it with your staff and board.

Stage 2. Risk Identification and Assessment

Once you've laid the groundwork for an ERM planning process, it's time to identify and assess risks (Figure 2.3). Your risk assessment will identify broad categories of actual and potential risk in your organization, analyze their characteristics, and consider what could happen if these risks occur. The goal here is to identify risks or vulnerabilities that could grow into risks before they harm or interfere with the organization's ability to do its work.

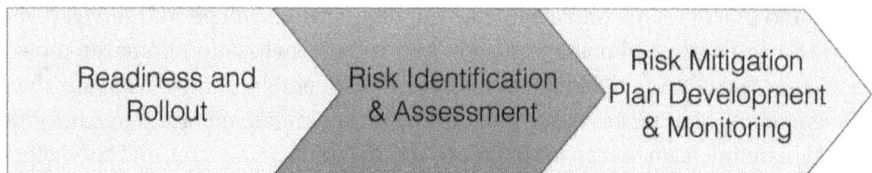

Figure 2.3: Risk Identification & Assessment

The specific goals of this phase are to:
–   Identify your organization's risks and vulnerabilities and categorize them by organizational function
–   Determine the severity of risk
–   Assess the possibility of recurrence and impact of risk
–   Prioritize key risks needing mitigation
–   Consider the drivers of risk
–   Create a Risk List
–   Create a Top 10 Risk List
–   Develop an outline for your ERM plan

Step 1. Risk Identification

Start with a mix of general framing and specific questions to guide your thinking and begin to surface issues, patterns, or trends. This section offers four approaches you can take to identify the risks that matter for your organization.
–   *Look for risks that affect most nonprofits.* Consider common financial, programmatic, operating, and compliance risks that are frequently found in nonprofit organizations and those in your specific field. There are risks that can affect all nonprofits and risks that are specific to the kind of work you do.
–   *Identify critical risks in your organization and flesh out your risks.* Add organization-specific risks to your list. You can use the Risk Details template or the app to capture the risks you have identified.
–   *Organize risks.* Categorizing risks will help you determine priorities for mitigation and action.
–   *Create a Top 10 Risk List.* This is a quick way to engage your team in risk identification and assessment. For smaller organizations or organizations that want to begin a risk management process quickly, this may generate the risk detail you need and you can move to Stage 3, "Building Your ERM Mitigation Plan." For organizations taking a long view or risk management, this can be an opening exercise with your team to jump-start the process.

In this section, you will find several tools to help you organize your risk assessment activities and makes sense of your findings.

Resources for Nonprofit Risk Identification

All nonprofit organizations and NGOs are required to meet certain government requirements around operations, board responsibilities and structure, financial management, and fundraising activities. These framing statutory or regulatory requirements offer a first look at possible areas of risk. US nonprofits are required to have whistle-blower protection policies that shield employees and volunteers from retaliation for reporting waste, fraud, or abuse. This includes a confidential reporting channel, investigation of the allegation, no repercussions to the reporter, and stringent document preservation and retention requirements. Additionally, annual conflict of interest reporting by board and staff, establishment of an audit committee, board review of the organization's 990 or other tax forms prior to submission, strong internal controls, as well as up-to-date policies including a written investment policy, a process for setting executive compensation, handling real estate transactions, annual independent audits with an exit conference, and making audits, tax forms, and fundraising practices available to the public. In the US, new FASB requirements will change how nonprofits do their accounting and reporting.

California, New York, the United Kingdom and other jurisdictions have stringent standards for nonprofits and charities operating there. A good starting point for your ERM plan is a frank assessment of your organization practice and compliance with national, state, regional, county, province, or local rules.

Organizations like BDO, FMA, Imagine Canada and Deloitte offer useful online resources on nonprofit and NGO risk. Another go-to resource includes standard-setting organizations that focus primarily on risk in commercial enterprises. While not identical to the risks facing nonprofits or NGOs, the standards are relevant; RIMS, CGMA, and COSO raise the bar for nonprofit risk management.

The International Classification of Nonprofit Organizations (INCPO) identifies 11 major groupings of nonprofits and NGOs: arts, culture and recreation, health and social services, environment, development and housing, education and research, advocacy, law and politics, philanthropy, international, religious, business, and professional associations. Check out online discussions of risk and industry conferences in your specialty area to broaden the scope of your review.

Getting Started with a Top 10 List

Ask your ERM team of board members, managers, staff, and volunteers to identify risks in their areas of responsibility. You can ask them to identify a single key risk or multiple risks. If there is consensus about the risks identified, you can prioritize them and create a Top 10 list. This exercise offers an opportunity to begin talking seriously about risk. It will heighten awareness of risks across the organization and build a shared sense of responsibility for developing solutions. Smaller organizations may find that a Top 10 Risk List will take you to the limits of your organization's resources for risk management. In this case, you can jump to Stage 3 and begin building your ERM mitigation plan outlined in Chapter 3.

Look for Common Nonprofit Risks

To get started thinking about nonprofit risk and what risk looks like in your organization, we've compiled a list of frequently occurring nonprofit risks. Not all nonprofits or NGOs have these vulnerabilities, but the list may prompt you to think about things to watch out for. Some of these risks are unique to nonprofits, but others occur in all kinds of businesses. Consider the list to kick-start your thinking about risks your organization may face.

- Fundraising/Marketing activities
    - Use of donor-restricted funds for a different purpose
    - Unauthorized use of the organization name or logo
    - Limited reputation management and media monitoring processes
- Government audits and investigations
    - Poor tracking of government contracts
    - Low rating on government performance scorecards
- Data protection and cyber security
    - Staff using personal e-mail for work-related communications
    - Data breach of client, staff, or donor personal information
- Program
    - Failure to maintain privacy and confidentiality
    - Inappropriate contact between staff and clients/participants
    - Complaints from clients/participants
    - Client/Participant safety
- Staffing/Personnel
    - Sexual harassment
    - Sleeping or intoxication on the job
    - Staff turnover
    - Late payment of employee benefits
    - No annual Executive Director performance and compensation review
- Volunteers
    - Poorly defined responsibilities and blurred roles for staff and volunteers
    - No background checks completed for assignments working with cash, children, youth or vulnerable adults
- Financial management
    - Irregular board or executive review of financials
    - Poor investment returns
    - Management of petty cash, purchase cards, or credit cards
    - Personal use of petty cash
    - Theft of funds
    - Accounting practices
- Facility/Space
    - Workplace injuries
    - Fire/safety violations
    - Unused leased space
    - No disaster emergency plan

- Other Operations
  - o   Theft or loss of food, supplies or equipment
  - o   Noncompliance with charity bureau or government regulations
  - o   Incomplete/inaccurate information on activities, finances, or operations
  - o   No annual conflict-of-interest training
  - o   Frequent company auto accidents
  - o   Complaints from neighbors

Step 2. Risk Assessment

How vulnerable is your organization to risk? Identifying risk is only part of the story. You need to weigh risks to decide which are priorities and warrant immediate attention, and which could have outsize effects on your organization. In most nonprofits, risk clusters on the service and program side of the house and in the finance area. But risk is also found in other functional areas of the organization where leaders are far less likely to take note and where fewer processes are in place to identify vulnerabilities or exposure.

When moving from risk identification to risk assessment, start from what you know and what you worry about. Think about the things that keep you up at night—what we call your worry list.
- What external and internal risks do you often see in your organization?
- What risks have you seen or heard about in other organizations?
- That risk can't happen here... or can it?
- What does your experience and data tell you about risks in your organization?
- What story does the risk data tell you?

Risk assessment looks at what risks or vulnerabilities are present in the organization or its operating environment. Risk can surface in all nonprofit organizations and in any department, program, or operational function. When risk emerges, it is typically due to a breakdown, lapse, or omission in one or more of the key operating pillars of an organization. These key pillars include your people, policies, practices, business processes, and technology.

People. Do you have the right people in the right jobs? Are your programs and operations staffed by people who can perform at or above expectations in their jobs? Do you have a sufficient number of staff and supervisors to perform critical activities? How do you handle human error or mistakes? How do you supervise and support staff and volunteers to prevent fraud, collusion, inefficiency, theft, inappropriate behavior, or poor performance? Does your organization have a code of ethics and statement of values?

Policies. Are the organization's rules and protocols formalized in writing and clearly and regularly communicated to staff, board, and recipients? How do you test for comprehension, understanding, and implementation? Are program and department manuals current and do staff members receive an orientation and annual refresher training? Do you update your policies annually to reflect current conditions, regulatory or industry changes, and new services or revenue streams? Do your policies include notification and escalation processes, internal controls, and supervisory sign-off? Do you have a risk policy?

Practices. Is practice consistent from person to person in your program, department, or division? How does your organization prepare employees and volunteers to think about risk, quality, and performance? How do you train, supervise, modify, correct, or use progressive discipline to improve performance and effectiveness and to reduce risk?

Processes. Are your business processes formalized and standardized? Do they flow from your policies? Do you have a notification and escalation process for critical information, untoward events or incidents? Does everyone understand the decision-making processes? Does your organization have a formal process for identifying, addressing, and tracking risk in each program, division, or department?

Technology. What technology solutions can you use to identify risk? Do you use automated financial management, talent management systems, electronic case records, or purchase cards? Are your data systems linked or tied to a quarterly dashboard report? How do you use the data you collect to identify areas of risk or issues to be addressed? Do you have a sensitive data inventory (where data is kept, acceptable use, records retention, encryption, security) and disaster recovery system?

In any risk assessment, the organization must evaluate an array of factors that might lead or contribute to a loss or claim or otherwise contribute to exposure.

Here are some tips to consider as you begin your risk assessment process:
- You can start with a focus on programs and services or risks to clients or participants, as these are the reason your organization exists, but your enterprise risk assessment efforts cannot stop there.
- Dive quickly into organizational operations asking a series of questions to assess risk awareness, risk tolerance, appetite for ERM, biggest worries (What trends are worrisome? What risks could deeply damage your organization? Where are improvements needed?), and what drives or causes risk.
- Take a hard look at government contracts and other legal or regulatory requirements. Have you submitted reports, claims, or data in a timely manner? Are your operating licenses current?

–   Dig deep into your data reports and data system capabilities: Is your organization automated or paper-driven? How do you collect and use data? Are reports available regularly? Do all staff and board see them? Are they easy to read and understand? Is the overall data quality reliable and accurate? Does the data capture processes, activities, and deliverables? Be on the lookout for gaps, such as departments or programs with no data.

–   Begin noting which risks are internal or external. Does the source of risk come from your people, practices, programs, policies, technology, or organization structure or does it come from regulations, contracts, the environment or the community?

–   Begin thinking about the likelihood and impact of the risks you've identified. For each identified risk, consider whether it's an ongoing vulnerability. Consider the degree of harm the risk could cause.

Identify and Flesh Out Your Risks

Once you've considered risks that typically affect nonprofits and NGOs, turn your focus to the risks in your own organization. Ask your division heads, department heads, and program managers to identify key risks in their areas of responsibility. They should look to their own staff, operations, and activities to uncover current or potential risks. Encourage them to follow smoke signals—hints that something is amiss. They should work from experience to identify risks that threaten to derail their operations and add details to flesh out the *categories* and *dimensions of risk* discussed briefly in Chapter 1.

–   Organize risks by grouping them into categories that reflect functional areas of operations.

–   Assess the likelihood of occurrence, recurrence, and impact a risk would have on operations.

–   Determine the severity and mix of risks.

–   Look for places where risks cluster.

–   Determine the likely cause or driver of the risk.

–   Think about the capacity and resources needed to address and resolve the risk.

–   The Risk Matrix model and the Risk Detail template and app are easy-to-use tools to help you identify and flesh out your risks.

Step 3. Organize and Describe Risks

Create a taxonomy to categorize your organization's risk by function, department, division, and program. Remember that risk occurs in all corners of nonprofit and NGO operations. Use the taxonomy to group similar risks under a single broad operational category. Look for risk in obvious and less obvious places. A standard nonprofit risk taxonomy covers all nonprofit operations and activities.

- Governance
- Programs and Staffing
- Volunteers
- Financial Management
- Fundraising
- Communications
- Environmental/Community Technology
- Facilities
- Operations/Administration

Throughout the book, we use the functional areas above as categories to illustrate where risks occur and how risk can emerge. There is a chapter dedicated to risks and risk considerations for each functional area.

To understand the origin of risk, your organization will engage in an exercise to pinpoint causal factors. The underlying factors that interact to create risk or the conditions in which risk can grow are called *drivers*. Use the five organizational pillars described previously in Step 2 (Risk Assessment) of this chapter as a framework to explore the forces that cause or restrain risk in your organization.

- *Policy.* Does the risk come from rules governing agency operations?
- *People.* Does the risk come from people and practice? Does it come from poor communication, limited supervision, weak feedback loops, or limited monitoring?
- *Process.* Does the risk come from business processes or protocols?
- *Technology.* Does the risk come from poor data quality, lack of information and analytic capacity, or hardware issues?
- *Structure.* Does the risk come from the organization of departments and functions, or from the management and supervisory hierarchy?

There are three other considerations that enrich understanding about the nature and importance of risk in nonprofits and NGOs: location, recurrence, and capacity to cure. Each of these considerations fleshes out your understanding of risk in your organization. They shed light on the dark corners of hidden or poorly understood risk to help you better understand what it will take to prevent or mitigate risk in your organization.

- Pinpoint the location of risk. Where did the risk occur or where is it likely to occur? What do you know about the program or department in which the risk occurred?
- Determine the department or program capacity to resolve the identified risk. What staff and other resources might be necessary to reduce risk?
- Determine whether you have identified an organization-wide risk, a single risk event, or a cluster of risks.
- Has the identified risk happened in one program, service, or department, or is it occurring or likely to occur in more than one location?

- Does the identified risk have a history or has it occurred before?
- Is it likely the risk will reoccur?

Tools for Risk Assessment

As we considered nonprofit risk, we wanted to develop an approach to ERM that would take the guesswork out of risk identification and assessment and put easy-to-use tools within reach for nonprofit leaders pressed for time. This section provides one model and two tools that you can use to make your own risk list and capture assessment detail and priority decisions. There are two primary tools for risk assessment: the Risk Details tool and the likelihood/impact matrix. You can use these tools from a paper template (Figure 2.4) or with an app like The Nonprofit Risk App (Figure 2.5).

Both on paper and in the app, you start with your risk list. On paper, you can populate the template with your list of risks and vulnerabilities, as shown in Figure 2.4. You may want to start thinking about a Top Ten list of risks now. As you see in the form on Figure 2.4, you can list your risks in two columns where the first column includes a top 10 list for high priority risks. You can add columns as you need them.

In the app (Figure 2.5), you tap Edit at the top right to enter a new risk with the +. You can then use the disclosure triangle (the right-pointing arrow) to move to details for the risk as you see in Figure 2.5 right. There you can select the items that are most likely to be causes of the risk and the ones that are most likely to be needed for mitigation.

Another feature of the Risk Details tool is its ability to help you capture your impression of your capacity to resolve the issue. The final section of the Risk Details tool lets you summarize the solution as it appears at this point. (Remember that with the app, you can always come back and change things as you get more information.).

Completing the Risk Details tool puts you on the road to mitigation planning, which is covered briefly here and in greater detail in Chapter 3.

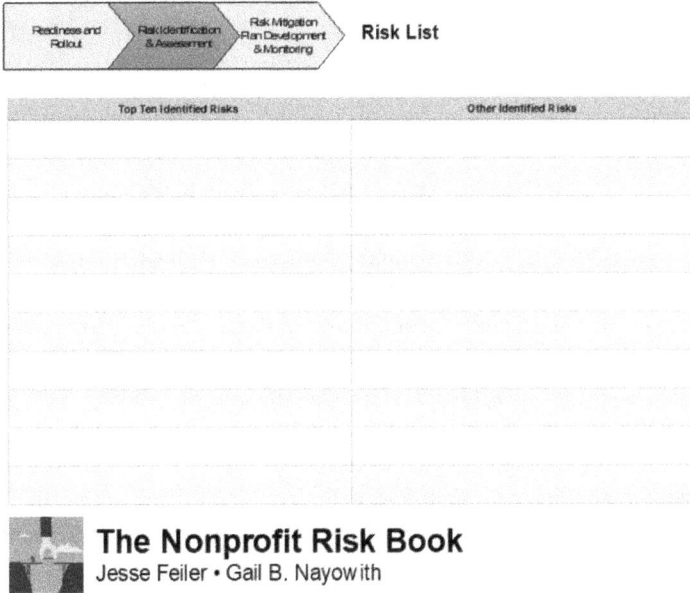

Figure 2.4: Risk List (Paper)

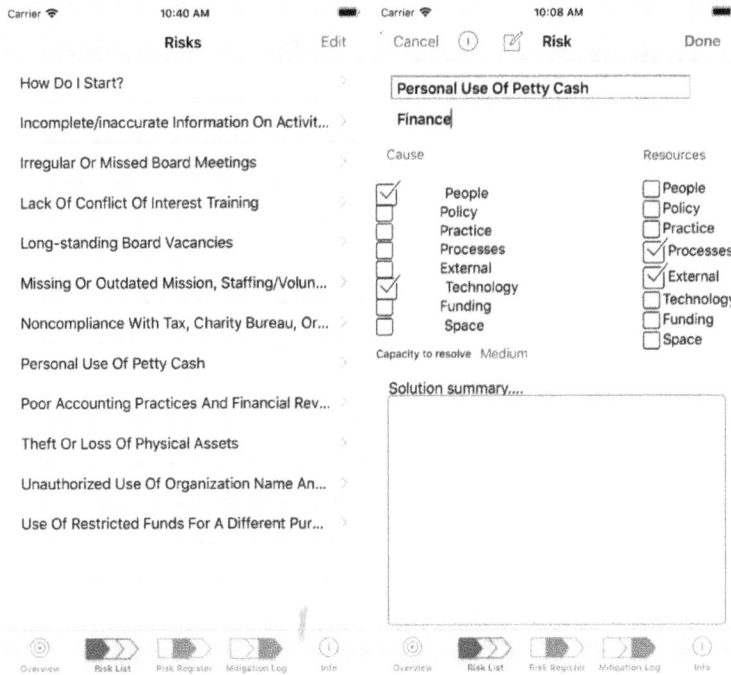

Figure 2.5: (left) Risk list. (right). Risk Details (Nonprofit Risk App)

Likelihood/Impact Matrix

Likelihood and impact are two dimensions used to assess the degree of harm that can result if a risk in your organization is not addressed. Likelihood is defined as the probability that a risk has, can, or will occur in the organization. The likelihood rating ranks the risk as very likely, moderately likely, or not very likely to occur. Impact is defined by how significant the effects of the risk could be on the organization. It answers the question of how serious the consequences would be if this risk occurred. Would the risk have a high, medium, or low impact?

You can use a two-by-two matrix like the one shown in Figure 2.6 to rank the risks on your list according to likelihood and impact. You take the risks identified in your Risk List and, in a discussion with your team, place each risk in the box that reflects your best thinking on the probability and effect it would have on your organization. Each box in the matrix corresponds to a scaled value, one that runs from high-to-low likelihood and another that runs from high-to-low impact. There is no single right way to forecast the likelihood or estimate the impact of risk. It helps to have your team involved in this exercise to add perspective and offer differing points of view.

Reaching team consensus on risk likelihood and impact will help you make decisions about resources needed and mitigation strategies with confidence. Figure 2.6 illustrates how a Likelihood/Impact Matrix might be completed by a nonprofit or NGO. The risk matrix tool answers the question: how vulnerable is your organization to risk?

	High Likelihood	Low Likelihood
High Impact	• Human resources practice • Incident reporting practice • Staff competencies and satisfaction • Government contract management • Data management, analysis & reporting • Fundraising revenue • Quality, performance, and risk monitoring	• Financial practice/internal audit • Press/Media • Crisis, disaster and business continuity planning • Leadership transition/succession planning • Cyber threats
Low Impact	• Facility considerations • Policies and procedures • Site support	• Board governance oversight • Government policy and policy shifts • Function integration of remote sites

Figure 2.6: Using the Likelihood/Impact Matrix

Moving to ERM Mitigation Planning

ERM is not a one-time activity. To build a culture that is risk aware, open about communicating risk concerns, and actively engaged in risk mitigation, everyone in the organization needs to become fluent in the language, meaning, and consequences of risk and understand their own role in risk management.

Risk activities are actions taken to cure or reduce the effects of an identified risk. It's the place where the organization decides what needs to be done to reduce, eliminate, or prevent risk from occurring or recurring. There are only a few ways to mitigate risk and these approaches can be used individually or in tandem, depending on the nature of the risk involved and your organization's capacity and resources available. The choices are clear-cut:

– *Eliminate the risk.* The organization can decide to eliminate the practice that is causing risk.
– *Mediate the risk.* You can mediate the risk through changes in policy, practice, technology, or people. This includes the development or revision of operating policies, enhancements to existing training and supervisory activities, new or enhanced technology solutions, personnel changes, or changes in business process and practice.
– *Track and monitor performance.* Mitigation monitoring includes an ongoing review of the completion and effectiveness of risk mitigation plan activities. Risk mitigation monitoring assesses the effectiveness of the activities put in place to reduce, eliminate, or prevent risk. Risk monitoring most often includes a review of key performance and risk indicators, validation checks like internal audits, or policy and practice spot-checks in non-financial areas of operation.

There are usually multiple methods to cure an identified risk and you can decide to use more than one approach to address the identified risk. Sometimes the risk can be mitigated by a change in business processes or the way things are done. It can also be mitigated by training, increased supervision, or developing a policy or business process where one does not exist.

This is best done through:
– Biannual ERM planning
– Monthly risk event review
– Quarterly risk mitigation review
– Adding an ERM focus to other quality and performance enhancing activities
– Regular reporting on risk mitigation activities alongside quality and performance improvement activities
– Board, staff, and volunteer training and refreshers

Risk mitigation monitoring is a check-in process for reviewing the status and completion of risk reduction activities. Risk event monitoring usually occurs monthly as part of an organization's quality and performance monitoring activities or as a standalone meeting. Risk mitigation monitoring typically occurs quarterly and with a yearly summary report of organization-wide performance and trends. All risk monitoring involves a review of planned activities and relevant data and a determination of whether the identified risk has been reduced, eliminated, or prevented.

Your ERM plan is the one document that lists:
- Identified organizational risks to be addressed
- The mitigation strategies or activities that will be undertaken to deal with each risk identified
- The desired goal that will come if the risk is dealt with properly
- Performance indicators that support effective risk mitigation
- The owner or person(s) responsible for implementing the risk mitigation activity, and the due date for completion

In Chapter 3, we will cover the steps for transitioning your risk assessment to an ERM plan and take you through plan development, tracking, and resolution activities.

Summary

This chapter shows you how to begin your ERM project and how to take the first concrete steps to identify and assess risks. In the following chapter, you will move on to manage and mitigate risks.

Chapter 3
Risk Mitigation Plan Development & Monitoring

The nonprofit management and capacity-building literature includes case study after case study of why corporate compliance, annual independent audits, and adequate insurance coverage only take a nonprofit organization so far when it comes to risk and sustainability. It prompted us to ask why so few nonprofits focus proactively on risk. For one thing, we found that nonprofit leaders rarely have the inclination or expertise to take on risk work on top of their other responsibilities. The tight budgets and limited bandwidth found in most nonprofit organizations, and the volatile environment in which they operate, called out for a written guide and online tools.

We wrote this book because so many nonprofit and NGO leaders worry about risk, but feel ill-equipped to address it. Executives say that they are more comfortable working from a quality improvement or performance management mindset because it speaks to organizational strengths, not vulnerability and weakness. Even a compliance environment seems to be easier for executives to engage because regulations, while often constraining and bureaucratic, are imposed externally and require little guesswork. The psychology of risk management requires personal and professional exploration of your own risk tolerance. It also requires an ability to accept the limits that your own history and experience places on the amount of risk you are willing to carry in the workplace. It comes from a deep understanding and acceptance that running a nonprofit means that you are in charge but not in control.

Our goal with this book is to take some of the risk out of risk management and make it easier for nonprofit leaders to do enterprise risk management. We want to help nonprofit leaders reduce the amount of time spent responding to and worrying about risk, increase efficiency when working with a consultant on a risk management project, and reduce the frustration that comes from having to build and implement a risk management system from scratch and with no guidance.

In this chapter, we get serious about risk management and monitoring. In Figure 3.1, you can see how risk management and monitoring fit into an overall ERM process.

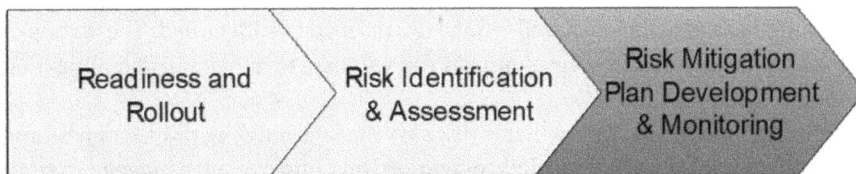

Figure 3.1: Risk Mitigation Plan Development & Monitoring

DOI 10.1515/9781501505942-003

Risk management and monitoring activities flow naturally from the work you've done so far to identify and understand risk in your organization. This chapter will help you get started with mitigation planning and detail the steps you need to take to reduce risk and exposure that could derail your operations and best laid plans. By the end of this chapter, you will be able to tie risks to solutions and construct and implement a customized ERM plan using a paper template or app.

Let's recap the process so far. You've identified and prioritized the risks you will address in your ERM Plan. You have a Top 10 list of the most important risks to mitigate (Figure 2.4). You've considered the organization's risk appetite—how much exposure, vulnerability, and uncertainty you can live with—and your staff capacity to resolve the identified risks (Figure 2.6). You've decided how much mitigation activity the organization can take on, and you know that actively managing key high-risk items will produce a better outcome than trying to handle every risk superficially and simultaneously. You've begun thinking about the kind of resources you will need to resolve the identified risks. Finally, you've been thinking about which program or department managers will be tasked with specific mitigation activities, who will be accountable for day-to-day mitigation work, and who will be responsible for putting solutions into place.

There are three parts to the ERM work at this stage:
- Turning your risk assessment into a risk mitigation plan (Figure3.1)
- Creating a risk register and risk mitigation log (Figure 3.4)
- Implementing your ERM plan and monitoring risk (Figure 3.5)

Turning Your Risk Assessment into a Risk Mitigation Plan

In designing risk mitigation strategies, the first rule of thumb is to figure out the simplest and most direct way of reducing or eliminating the risk. The second rule is to ensure that the solution proposed fits the risk and that it is likely to result in a measurable reduction in vulnerability or exposure. The third and final rule is to carefully consider the source and drivers of risk, whether it's a single, cluster, or organization-wide risk and whether it is likely to reoccur. The goal is to develop and implement a set of mitigation activities that will reduce the risks you've identified. These considerations will help you frame the approach you will take to mitigation and mitigation planning.

Developing an organization that is risk-savvy means building risk awareness and opportunities for mitigation into daily operations and into overall management strategy. An organization that values communication and disclosure will create multiple channels for staff, board, volunteers, recipients, and others to report incidents and situations of concern. Smart leaders will create systems that have reinforcing and redundant features. In the US, this is referred to as belts and suspenders practice. In the

UK, it's called belt and braces. These redundant and reinforcing processes are protective strategies established out of an abundance of caution to catch or minimize risk.

The idea is to create an ERM plan that fits seamlessly into your ongoing training, business processes, and other performance and quality improvement, oversight, and monitoring activities. Mitigation activities are recommended actions intended to fill in gaps caused by an organization's vulnerabilities. Focus on the risks your team has identified across all areas of operations—program, staffing, finance, administration/operations, fundraising, communications, governance, and those occurring externally. The mitigation activities you choose should aim to close the gap between organizational vulnerabilities and the operational capabilities needed to address them. Risk mitigation, quality, and performance improvement strategies work in tandem to reduce exposure and improve practice. Expect that risk assessment and mitigation strategy development will be ongoing with your formal ERM plan developed or refreshed every 18 to 36 months. Imagine a scenario where your organization has a standing monthly meeting to review and monitor specific incidents and performance and quality metrics and a quarterly meeting to review progress made on the ERM plan.

When you begin to craft solutions to the risks identified by your team, think about ways to adapt or revise policies, procedures, business processes, and protocols. Consider ways to train or supervise staff, keeping these risks in mind. Explore technology solutions as part of or as a companion to other risk mitigation activities.

- Revise or develop new policies and procedures
- Redesign business processes and protocols
- Develop technology solutions
- Include a focus on ERM when onboarding staff and volunteers and when orienting new board members
- Rethink staff and volunteer supervision and training

You'll want to build five foundational processes to support the implementation of your enterprise risk mitigation plan. Each process is discussed in detail below.

1. Draft an enterprise risk policy that describes the framework for ERM activities.
2. Use tools to develop Mitigation Action Plans (MAPs) to manage risk management activities.
3. Establish a reporting process to share information with managers and board members. Monitor the status and completion of risk mitigation activities.
4. Develop indicators to track risk, and summarize mitigation activities and document resolution.
5. Create a schedule for producing and distributing mitigation monitoring reports and for reviewing the effectiveness and completion of mitigation activities.

Step 1. Develop an Enterprise Risk Policy that Describes the Overall Framework for ERM Activities

Your ERM policy is the place where you lay out the organization's approach to risk and risk management. It codifies the standards governing organization risk practice—the way you'll do things—and lays out expectations of staff, board, volunteers, vendors, affiliates, and others. A strong ERM policy starts with a statement that the practice of identifying, assessing, managing, and mitigating risk is an organizational priority. It should include language noting that risk management is everyone's business. The policy should describe opportunities and outline the various channels for staff, managers, program participants, and board to report risk with no fear of reprisal. Your enterprise risk policy should cover all areas of organizational operations from programs and services to governance to finance and operations, from staffing to reputation and facility management, to a discussion of the external risks that affect agency operations. It should also reference an expectation of compliance with all laws, regulations, and organizational policies. The ERM policy statement should also explicitly acknowledge board and executive leadership accountability for actively managing risk and the tracking and oversight processes that will be used to monitor risk, risk mitigation, and risk resolution activities. Your ERM policy should also describe the internal control systems—the checks and reinforcing business processes—that will be used to manage risk. It should describe the escalation chain for notifying executive leadership and board of risk incidents and resolution. Finally, your ERM policy should delineate the rules under which your organization will operate its risk management activities. The ERM policy can be organized in a way that allows it to become a new section in your organization's operations manual or onboarding material.

The basic elements of your ERM policy should include a discussion of:
- *Risk Mitigation Philosophy and Goals.* Why does risk management matter? What do we hope to accomplish through enterprise risk management? What risk reduction or quality or performance improvement targets do we wish to set and reach?
- *Accountability Structure and Processes.* Who is responsible for identifying and managing risk?
- *Risk Committee Membership and Operations.* How will the committee operate? What reports and data will be produced and reviewed? What is the general operating framework for the committee?
- *Indemnification and Insurance Coverages.* This section should include a description of insurance coverages, indemnification parameters, and other relevant provisions.

- *Internal Audit and Compliance Monitoring and Validation Processes.* How will the organization ascertain adherence to the ERM policy? Will it include internal program and fiscal audits or spot checks? What methods will be used to test and validate whether risk reduction strategies are working?
- *Operating Policies and Requirements.* How will the ERM policy and activities interface with other organizational requirements, including annual independent audits, compliance with laws and regulations, quality and performance improvement activities and industry best practice? What methods will be used to review policies or operating manuals to keep them current?
- *Quality Improvement, Risk and Performance Tracking Reports and Activities.* What information will be collected? How it will be reported out? How will cross-program, department or affiliate comparisons be made? How will benchmarks and relevant industry standards be used? How will outliers be addressed?

Step 2. Use Tools to Develop Mitigation Action Plans (MAPs) to Manage Risk Management Activities

Use the Mitigation Action Plan template or app to detail the activities your organization will undertake to prevent, reduce, or manage your identified risks and provide status updates to the executive team and board ERM committee. There are a handful of mitigation management tools that can be employed when you identify risk in your organization. Typical mitigation options include staff training, supervision, adding or reassigning staff, clarifying staff functions, disciplinary action as a last resort, retooling a business process or practice, a department restructuring or program closure as a last resort, a technology fix, or reassessing your insurance needs.

Your mitigation action plan must create a straight path linking the problem to an actionable solution. Remember that the activities you select and tools you choose to use should measurably reduce the risk or vulnerability you've identified and document the reduction in a way that is easy to understand. The MAP template or app will prompt you to do this. Some risks can be mitigated by using one tool, although it's usually the case that a combination of tools will be needed to reduce an identified risk.

It's worth reinforcing the point that in addition to the ERM mitigation plan, your organization will want to establish a new process or enhance your existing incident monitoring activities. Incident review details and process should be delineated in your risk policy. Your incident reports should include the date of the incident, description of the situation, details on time of day, location, staff or recipients present or affected, immediate actions taken, proposed actions to be taken, expected outcomes, person responsible for implementing the corrective action, resources needed, validation method, and due date. Where incident management tracks the remediation of specific hazards with a goal of returning the organization to normal operations as quickly as possible, risk mitigation planning seeks to address root cause and assumes a portfolio view of risk across departments and programs.

Step 3. Develop a Reporting Process to Monitor the Status and Completion of Risk Mitigation Activities

The reporting process you develop will work optimally if it feeds into a quality, performance, or risk committee at the staff level, to a board committee such as a Compliance or Quality Improvement, or to a newly established Risk and Performance Committee. These committees will be responsible for monitoring the status of ERM mitigation efforts and tracking implementation of the ERM plan. To make it easier to track implementation and mitigation activities and to monitor risks, you will need to construct a set of indicators and develop a report or dashboard that will allow you to keep an eye on key operations and identify emerging risks. These indicators can be framed as key performance indicators (KPIs), key risk indicators (KRIs), or a combination of the two. Each indicator represents a potential risk. The indicators should capture essential activities, critical incidents, or performance gaps in each department or program. We discuss KPIs in detail below.

Your ERM plan and mitigation monitoring activities are only as good as your underlying business processes. Strong management and quality and performance management will reinforce the commitment to preventing and reducing risks. This two-part action is a necessary process redundancy that is referred to as a belt and suspenders or hook and net process. If you don't catch a vulnerability or weakness with one process, you'll catch it with another.

If you already have a strong quality and performance management system and use KPIs, you can add new operations indicators or develop an additional set of KRIs. We prefer the simplicity of a KPI framework because it names the goal for data collection and tracking: to make your organization stronger and less prone or susceptible to risk. Your KPIs should include metrics for each operating department, division, and program. You can use the same functional categories listed in Chapter 2 and detailed in Part II of this book. We'll quickly recap the functional categories here and offer some examples to prompt your thinking.

Monthly incident and performance review meetings align organizational goals and views of success across the organization. ERM monitoring meetings encourage discussion about progress toward organization-wide risk reduction goals. Both the monthly incident and performance review meetings and the quarterly ERM plan review meetings promote timely identification of emerging and deep-rooted risks. This process makes it possible to ground decision-making in data and facts. It enables comparison from year-to-year or across programs or affiliates. It creates a place to examine trends in performance, work flow or process gaps. It also helps everyone in the organization operate from the same base of information and develop a shared perspective on what works and what doesn't. Risk governance and risk awareness are reinforced by Board and staff committees and protocols. The cross-functional team like the one you tapped to do risk assessment can be tapped to manage the ERM and KPI data and generate reports. You will have to consider what data platform you will use to capture and present the data in report or dashboard form.

Step 4. Develop Indicators to Track and Report Risk, Summarize Mitigation Activities and Document Resolution

Key performance indicators (KPIs) serve as early warning alerts to catch vulnerabilities in programs or operations. They enable data-informed decision-making, offer a snapshot of current status, trends over time, and help you progress toward your goals. Using key indicators helps benchmark programs and operations and makes it easier to spot outliers that may need special attention. The indicators you choose need to be organization-wide. They can cascade down to programs and departments or to individual staff, as you choose. Using metrics changes an organization's culture. Metrics can be expected to change the way your board, managers, staff, and volunteers think and act.

The ERM plan outlines a series of mitigation activities that can be tracked and captured in data reports or dashboards over time.

- Develop risk and performance indicators to track progress made to reduce, prevent, or eliminate risk
- Develop reduction targets for each category of risk
- Collect and report data monthly, quarterly, and annually
- Identify positive and negative outliers across programs or departments
- Consider quarterly and year-over-year trends
- Establish organizational, department, and program benchmarks

When considering indicators you will want to answer these questions: What risk or performance questions do we want to answer? What do we need and want to know about our programs and operations? Do we already collect data that can be used to measure a reduction in risk? Can we get other meaningful data? Do we have a data source (technology platforms, surveys, interviews, focus groups, satisfaction surveys, journey mapping, research/evaluation, observation, attestation, peer-to-peer, qualitative, and quantitative data)? How reliable is our data and what data quality improvements are needed for it to be useful in tracking risk reduction?

There are many KPIs to consider. The key is to choose the fewest number of indicators needed to capture the main areas of quality, performance, and risk in your organization across all programs and departments. You can turn other indicators into data dashboards for program directors or department managers. The list below offers some indicators to consider as you think through your own short list of KPIs.

- Operations
  - Record-keeping and record retention practices meet industry standards.
  - Report on pending litigation, large insurance claims, payouts, settlements and disclosures are shared with the board annually.
  - A disaster-recovery plan is in place for all departments and programs.
  - Adequate insurance coverage is in place for each line of business.
  - Facility maintenance plans are current for all sites.
  - All facilities are in a state of good repair and all facility violations have been cured.
  - Program and department manuals are up to date.
  - Fleet management policies are current and a maintenance plan is in place.
  - Emergency and disaster recovery plans are current with staff trained in their use.
- Programs
  - Accreditations or licenses for all programs or facilities are up to date.
  - Program evaluation and impact data on some or all programs are shared with staff, board, funders, and the community.
  - A safety and incident management plan is in place for all programs and sites.
  - Services are fully enrolled and subscribed and data is available on program utilization and vacancies.
- Financial Management
  - Government contracts or foundation grants cover the cost of all program operations.
  - A current financial sustainability plan is in place.
  - The annual budget includes 3–6 months of cash reserves.
  - Fraud prevention activities and testing internal controls are operating in all programs and departments.
  - Audit findings are monitored for material deficiencies, significant findings, and business recommendations.
  - A Board- and auditor-approved expense allocation methodology is used in all programs and departments.
  - Board has reviewed and approved annual operating and capital budgets.
  - Quarterly reporting on revenue mix by source.
  - Financial reporting and presentation material meets industry standards.

- FASB, 990, and other government accounting and reporting practices are consistent with industry standards and submissions are complete.
- Line of credit accounting report is produced and distributed quarterly.
- Cash flow report is produced monthly for executive staff and quarterly for board.
- Quarterly report on cost per unit of service by program type is produced and distributed to executive staff and board.

- Staffing
  - All hiring processes meet fair labor and industry best practice standards.
  - Employee handbook is current and meets legal and industry standards.
  - Staff and leadership have the political acumen needed to manage programs, finances, contracts, and grants.
  - A code of conduct, organizational ethics, and values is distributed to all incoming staff, volunteers, and board members.
  - A succession plan for key positions is in place.
  - Staffing coverage ratios are maintained and reported for each program.
  - Compliance with fair labor practices.
  - Staff turnover or vacancy rates higher than 10% annually are tracked and reported for each program or department.
  - Background checks and clearances are conducted for all employees.
  - Annual corporate compliance training is completed by all employees.

- Governance
  - Bylaws are current and comply with local law and industry standards.
  - Completion rate of 100% for annual conflict-of-interest training and disclosure attestations.
  - Board-approved annual budget.
  - Regular meetings are held and decisions are made with a quorum present.
  - Investment policy is reviewed and updated annually.
  - Board approvals are given and recorded for contract execution, borrowing limits, spending approvals, and purchase or sale of building.
  - Annual performance and compensation reviews meets local standards for all executive staff.

- Fundraising and Communications
    - Charity review rating and organization reputation is monitored regularly.
    - Crisis communications plan is current.
    - Gap to actual funds raised and fundraising by source/type is reported quarterly.
    - Unfavorable press is tracked as a significant risk and reported to members of the executive team and board.
    - Annual fundraising expenses are below 35%.
- Environment
    - Community engagement activities are tracked and reported by type and activity.
    - Regular monitoring of changes in federal, state, regional, local regulations and legislation.
    - Advocacy activities are conducted in accordance with regulations and meet industry standards.
    - No political contributions are made with organization funds.
    - Weapons or active shooter policy is current and staff have received training.
- Technology
    - Cyber security policy is current and implemented in all departments and programs.
    - Data recovery plan is current and regularly tested.
    - Data privacy is maintained in all programs and departments and all breaches are disclosed timely.
    - Sufficient staff members are trained to enter data and produce reports from all data platforms.

Step 5. Create a Schedule for Monitoring ERM Plan Implementation and Reviewing the Effectiveness of Mitigation Strategies

Performance and progress on ERM plan implementation should be monitored monthly at the program and department levels. Summary reports should be provided to the executive team and board quarterly and annually, with year-to-date and year-over-year comparisons available. It can be useful to develop outlier reports to flag programs or departments where performance is well above or below the system-wide average. One rule of thumb is to use your fiscal year and board meeting calendars to establish reporting dates.

Creating a Risk Register and Risk Mitigation Log

Using the template or app is a quick way to build your ERM plan and mitigation status tracker. The template below offers an easy way to get started. The Risk Register tool allows you to capture your most important risks and risk assessment detail on the severity, importance and source to create a work plan for addressing them. Drop the Top 10 or your other priority risks into the risk register. The risk register and mitigation log show the source and severity of risks to be mitigated. It allows you to sequence the timing of mitigation activities, identify the risk owner and mitigation manager, and track mitigation implementation and completion dates. By documenting this risk detail, you are establishing parameters you can use to develop a mitigation plan for each risk.

Figure 3.2 shows a risk register you can download and use.

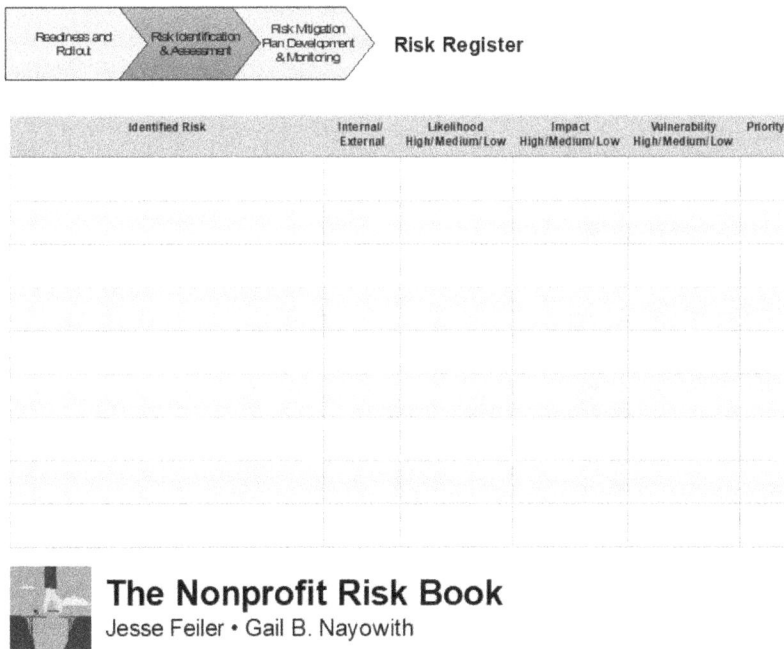

Figure 3.2: Using a Paper-Based Risk Register

If you use The Nonprofit App, the Risk Register has the same information; however, instead of multiple columns, buttons at the top let you sort and re-sort the data to focus each aspect of the risk as you see fit. You can see the app's risk register in Figure 3.3.

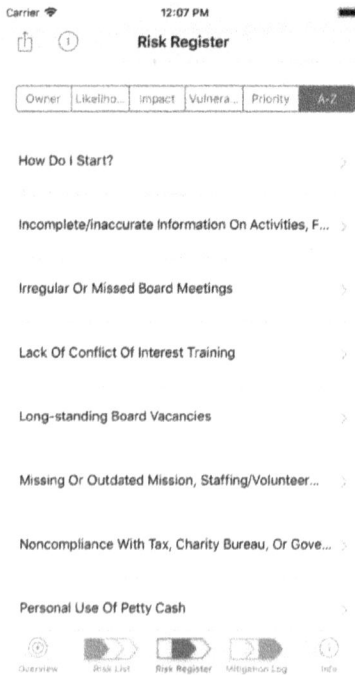

Figure 3.3: Using the Risk Register

The risk register is where your organization will determine the areas of risk you will explore, the source of the risk, the risk's likely effect on your organization, and the risks you will want to mitigate in this round of ERM planning. As a rough guide, you can start by using your top ten risks or including risks your team has identified in programs, finance and agency operations. Note whether the risk is internal or external, and the likelihood, impact, and vulnerability posed by each risk you've identified. Once completed, this template becomes the basis for your ERM plan.

After you identify and prioritize the risks you will mitigation in your ERM plan, you will want to move on to the Risk Mitigation Log. The log can be used to capture the set of activities you will undertake to reduce, prevent, or eliminate identified risks. It will also capture the methods you will use to track successful implementation, the lead person or responsibility owner, and a validation methodology for confirming successful completion or cure. You can use basic metrics to track progress made in implementing risk mitigation activities, and you can validate completion or cure through attestation, spot-checks, internal audit, document review, and site visits. Figure 3.4 shows the Risk Mitigation Log in the app.

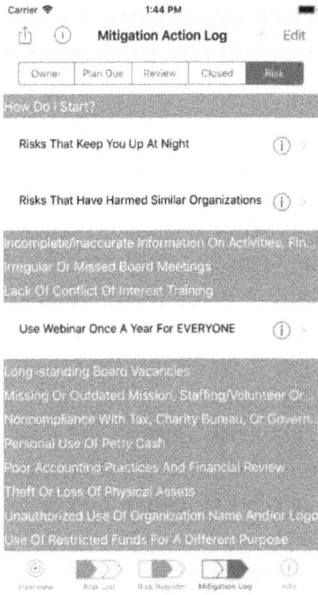

Figure 3.4: Risk Mitigation Log

Figure 3.5 shows the details for a single risk mitigation action from the log.

Figure 3.5: Mitigation Action Details

In thinking about the activities or strategies you will use to tackle risk in your organization, you will want to think carefully about your risk appetite and organizational risk tolerance. Will you be able to eliminate, reduce, or manage the risk with the planned activities? How will you or board feel if, after taking action, some element or degree of risk remains?

You will also want to attach a timeframe and an owner to each risk mitigation activity, as demonstrated in Figure 3.5. Who in the organization will be responsible for doing the work to reduce, eliminate, or manage the identified risk, or will you bring in outside experts to assist? When will the work start? How complex is the solution to implement? What are the cost and resource considerations for mitigating these risks? How long will it take to complete? What is the due date for completion?

Your risk register and mitigation log will capture a configuration of risks unique to your organization. It will be tailored to your needs, your risk appetite and tolerance, and to the capacity of your managers to implement. If dutifully implemented, this bespoke plan can be used for a period of up to three years to reduce, eliminate, or manage the risks you face.

Reporting and Mitigation Accountability Strategies

The ERM team will meet every month with owners of each risk, will check in at regular monthly, quarterly, and annual intervals, and attest to and provide data on progress made to reduce the risks identified in the ERM plan until goals are reached. At each check-in, the manager or risk owner should describe activities undertaken to reduce or mitigate the risk. Validation activities like spot-checks, internal audit, and program or document reviews can test for the absence or reduction of identified risks and adjustments can be made to amend the mitigation strategy as needed. A final test at completion completes the mitigation.

A Note on Residual Risk

Organizations cannot eliminate risk completely. Carefully crafted mitigation strategies and actively managed implementation will allow you to reduce risk to an acceptable level.

Implementing Your ERM Plan and Monitoring Risk

There are five phases to an ERM plan implementation:
- *Securing agreement on the organization's risk profile.* You and your ERM team must share a consistent view about risk and agree to model and reinforce it with

staff, volunteers, affiliates, and vendors. This means that you have established parameters about risk appetite, risk tolerance, and risk policy. You have identified, narrowed down and arrived at consensus on the priority risks to be addressed in your ERM plan. You and your team have agreed on desired mitigation activities and owners responsible for each identified risk, and you have agreed to a deadline date for completion of risk mitigation activities.

- *Arriving at clarity about the organization's risk management, governance structure, and management responsibilities.* Strong risk management practice starts with the tone set at the top. The executive team and board leadership have roles to play in increasing risk awareness and management within the organization.

- *Entering the agreed upon list of organizational risks and risk events to be mitigated in the Risk Register and Risk Mitigation Log.* Your ERM project manager can be tasked with managing the ERM work. This individual is responsible for constructing the ERM plan with agreed upon ERM tools, and for managing the ERM initiative. Your ERM team, in conjunction with your program and department heads, can use one or several monthly ERM meetings to refine the list of identified risks to a number that your organization can act on effectively. You can use the Risk Register template or app to capture and rank risks and select those your organization chooses to mitigate.

- *Agreement on risk mitigation activities to prevent, reduce, or eliminate risk.* Your ERM team and department and program managers can use one or more of the monthly meetings to craft mitigation solutions for each identified risk. Remember that the mitigation activity should produce a discernible and measurable reduction in the risk it is intended to address.

- *Continuous tracking of internal and external risk events, enhanced reporting and monitoring of risk and performance, and biannual ERM plan updates.* The timeframe for your ERM plan can stretch over an 18- to 36-month period, depending on resources and other organizational priorities. It is best to get your organization on a regular cycle of ERM planning and to keep your risk register current and mitigation plan updated. Extending beyond a three-year timeframe on any mitigation activity adds its own risks. For most nonprofit organizations, the pace of change is too fast and the consequences of failing to keep up are too great to adopt a long-term view of risk. Conditions on the ground in your programs, operations, or community served; your plans for growth, consolidation, or cutbacks and progress made on your strategic goals—anything that shifts or changes your work will create new pockets of risk that need attention. Similarly, changes in the funding, legislative, or regulatory environment, or social and political climates pose risks if left unexamined and unaccounted for.

Summary

Successful ERM plan implementation is completely dependent upon the tone set at the top and upon a regular pattern of reinforcing communication, training, supervision, performance reviews, and data sharing. Information and accountability are the cornerstones of effective ERM.

This chapter provides you with details for the various steps to take in your plan. In Chapter 4, we will walk you through other ERM planning tools and how to use them. By the end of the chapter, you will have an idea of whether using a paper or online tool is right for you, your team, and your organization. You can start testing the tools by entering your own data. The remaining chapters of *The Nonprofit Risk Book* focus on risks in key areas of operations and the backbone of your organization.

Chapter 4
Making It Work

The previous chapters describe the risk assessment, planning and management process and the rationale behind it. This chapter recaps and walks you through the details of putting those concepts into action.

You've already taken the first step by starting to think about organization risks and vulnerabilities and what you can do about them. There are many ways to move forward, but the most important thing to bear in mind is to do just that: move forward. Your organizational culture and the conditions that led to your decision to begin ERM planning will drive the pace, depth and scope of your ERM work. Sometimes ERM projects start because an organization has suffered a catastrophic event or critical incident and leaders are determined never to go through that again. Often, the experience of a peer organization or another nonprofit is observed or reported in the press and this prompts reflection and the need for focused self-assessment and preventive mitigation.

ERM planning can even be undertaken when a nonprofit is starting up or when there is a transition in executive leadership or because a board member has a concern. Whether you begin ERM planning to give your new organization a healthy start, recover from a bad situation, refresh longstanding policy or better align strategy and practice, thoughtful ERM planning can help your organization reach its goals.

Regardless of the initiating event, the most important point is to get started, and this chapter can help you do that.

Tip: If you are starting with a limited project, try not to pick the simplest area of your organization nor the most complex one.

Getting Started

The process you are embarking on is basically linear, as the diagram shown in Figure 4.1 (and others in this book) shows.

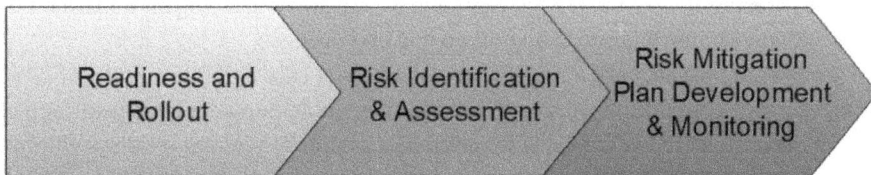

Figure 4.1: Overview of the Risk Management Process

DOI 10.1515/9781501505942-004

You'll see the diagram shown in Figure 4-1 throughout the book (and in The Nonprofit Risk App as well). It's a reminder of the process that you'll build to find and manage risk in your nonprofit organization. The process steps we outline will help guide you along the way. You begin with getting ready and rolling out the project in your organization. This process is critically important as you identify a project manager or hire a consultant to facilitate and start to assemble a team that will be working together for a period of time. Once your team is assembled, you can move on to identifying the risks to which your organization may be exposed. As you identify each risk, you assess its cause and significance: how likely it is to happen (once or repeatedly) and how much damage could it do. Risks are then categorized and ranked so that your planning work centers on the highest priority risks.

With your risks identified, assessed and prioritized, you move on to the third step, which is to develop mitigation strategies for each identified risk, implementing those strategies and monitoring the effects of your mitigation activity.

If you are thinking about assessing risk in your nonprofit organization, there are several strategies you can use. One way is to use benchmarks or metrics to compare your organization and its risks with peer organizations and see how your organization lines up against an industry standard. This is useful when a nonprofit organization has a strong quality and performance management process in place and several years of clean data. This approach allows an organization to set risk reduction goals and measure progress against a target. One challenge is that comparable benchmark data is hard to find for nonprofit organizations across all areas of programming and operations.

The other approach, which is the one we take in *The Nonprofit Risk Book*, is to help leaders work with the resources they have and know best: their own data and experience. To that end, we suggest areas for you to consider and pursue in your risk assessment effort, but our emphasis is on *your* organization. While it's valuable to compare your organization with others, your attention and primary focus must be on developing an ERM risk mitigation plan and processes for your own organization.

There is one universal aspect of risk that holds for all organizations and it's one you should keep top of mind: You are not alone in your worry about risk management, and you're not the first to have to impose the discipline of ERM planning on a nonprofit organization. In talking with nonprofit executives and boards we have heard these worries expressed in countless meetings and as confidential requests for help and guidance. A board member or colleague reports a bad incident or operational crisis in wrenching detail believing that their organization is facing an unsurmountable challenge or terrible situation that no one else ever has.

In listening we are very often able to put minds at ease and see the weight lifted from their shoulders when we say, "Yes, this same thing happened two years ago at XYZ organization." Fortunately, it is rare that a nonprofit nightmare arises with no warning and rarer still when catastrophe strikes in an entirely new way.

As we thought about the heavy weight of shame and isolation carried by executives and board members in the face of what is most often a consequence of nonprofit program operations and business models, we developed an even greater appreciation for the need to open up conversations about risk and risk management to make it as commonplace as conversations about other nonprofit management activities. We've taken these conversations to heart and offer an approach to risk management aimed at helping executives and boards find and fix vulnerabilities while they are still small and well before they grow into disasters.

Although it is basically linear, as you proceed with the ERM planning process you may realize that some changes need to be made, so you can easily revisit an earlier process point. It can be tempting in an effort like this to force it to be sequential with every step completed before proceeding to the next. Most planning and implementation processes move forward and back on the way to completion as new information emerges or conditions change. This said, planning projects cannot go on indefinitely and the beauty of plans is that once they are completed, anything left out can be added in at a later date or picked up in the next plan. The timeframe for your ERM planning process should be finite so that you don't get caught in an endless feedback loop or the trap known as paralysis by analysis.

In order to move forward quickly, you will need a way of working that accommodates to the changes you will experience as you rollout and implement your ERM plan. There are two ways you can do that.

- *The Nonprofit Risk App.* You can use The Nonprofit Risk App, which is downloadable from the App Store. It's designed for a nonlinear approach so that you can move through your project as you need to.
- *Forms.* Use modifiable media such as paper, spreadsheets, and smart boards to manage the project. You might consider downloading the forms that we have shared in previous chapters in this book. You can download them as PDF files, or print copies as you need them. The URL for downloads is champlainarts.com/nprisk/forms.

Some people prefer to work digitally, while others prefer to work on paper, so you can choose what you're most comfortable with. If you compare the two methods, you'll see that paper forms let you enter all of your data on grids or spreadsheets. With an app, you enter the data into smaller sections, and the app puts the data together according to your choices when you want to view it.

This structure allows the app to change the display as needed. For example, consider the risk mitigation log shown in Figure 4.2. As is the case throughout the Nonprofit Risk app and many other apps, the data is presented first as a list (such as the list of mitigation actions on the left of Figure 4.2). You can tap the pointed disclosure arrow at the right of each item in the list to see its details, as you see on the right of Figure 4-2. When you use the disclosure arrow or Info circle to look at details, you'll find a Back button at the top left of the details screen. Use that to return to the list view. (You'll see it at the top left of Figure 4.2 right.)

Taken together, the mitigation log in the app lets you enter dates for the creation of a Mitigation Action Plan (MAP), its review, and its completion. The app reminds you of upcoming MAP dates both within the app and (if you choose) by sending you notifications with whatever lead time you want.

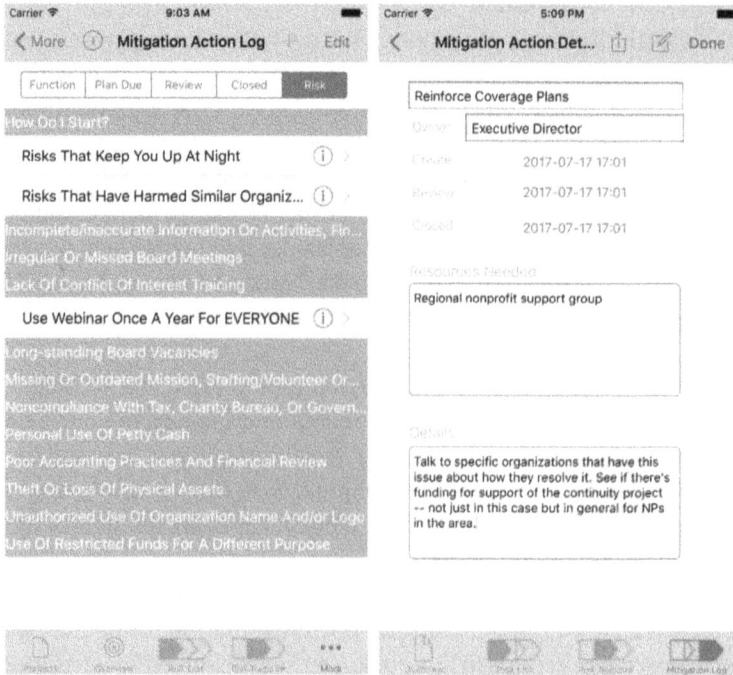

Figure 4.2: Mitigation Action Log (left) and Details (right)

With paper, the format for capturing your data is basically set when you choose your form. If you are undecided about whether to go with a paper or app tool for your ERM process, experiment with one hypothetical risk using the downloadable paper form, and try it again with the app. This will not only help you make your choice, but it will also get you into the routine of looking at risks so that you're ready when you actually start your own non-hypothetical project.

The Nonprofit Risk App

The Nonprofit Risk app functionality parallels this book. When you launch the app for the first time, you will see an overview of your project. If you have opened the app for the first time, you will have an empty project to work with. An overview for a project in progress is shown in Figure 4.3.

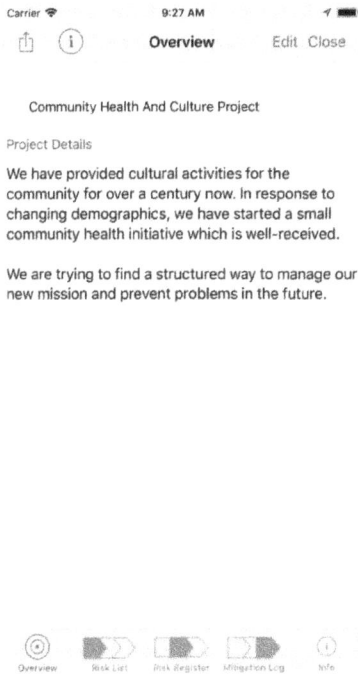

Figure 4.3: Overview

Navigation Bar (Top Controls)

Each screen in the app has controls at the top and bottom. In Figure 4.3, the controls at the top are, from right to left:

- *Close Button.* Available only on the overview, this button closes your current project and lets you create or open a new one.
- *Edit Button.* When this is tapped, you are able to edit the data in the current project. Some controls are dimmed at this point. The Edit button's name is changed to Done, and a Cancel button appears at the left of the top toolbar. When you tap either Done or Cancel, your changes are saved or discarded and all controls are re-enabled.
- *To the left of the title there may be a Notes button with a pencil and pad.* This lets you enter notes and comments on almost every screen. If you have entered notes, this button will be highlighted.

- *To its left, is an Info button.* This shows a popover with a summary of navigation commands and a link to get more information about using the app.
- *Further left is a Share button—a box with an arrow pointing up.* This enables you to share the data on the screen via e-mail, Messages, the Notes app, and other apps you may have installed. If a printer is available, you will be able to print the data.

Tab Bar (Bottom Controls)

At the bottom of the view, you'll see tabs you can use to navigate. The current control is highlighted. The buttons for the Risk List, Risk Register, and Mitigation Log are small versions of the images you see in this book. The Info button at the bottom provides background information about the app and about us.

Note: The figures in this chapter are illustrative of the process. They do not represent a completed risk management process; that would be substantially larger.

Readiness and Rollout

Once you decide on using the app or paper template, you're ready to begin the project as shown in Figure 4.4.

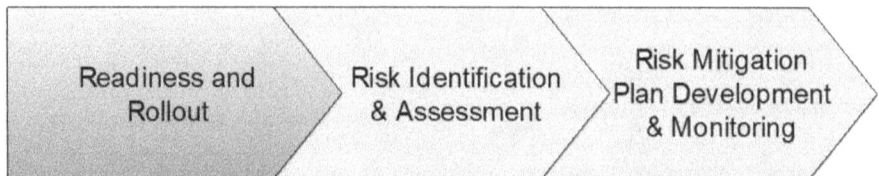

Figure 4.4: Readiness and Rollout.

The methods needed to activate the readiness and rollout stage in an ERM process are tools you already have and use: research, training, meetings, persuasion, memos, newsletters, social, and anything other channels you and your organization use to communicate and engage with your staff, managers, volunteers, service users and board.

The more you inform and engage your organization in thinking about risk and risk awareness, the better your plan will be. Broad-based support and buy-in will strengthen the ERM work and the ERM planning project. A mandate handed down from "on high" may not be the way you typically start change projects in your organization, but an enthusiastic embrace of risk management by leaders from the start is a necessary signal that this work is valued and a priority. It's unusual that ERM has to be mandated and closed to discussion, but in cases of significant resistance, the process may need a kick start.

It is useful to keep an eye out for outright opposition to the project. Opposition may come from people who are simply averse to change, or it may come from people who feel specifically threatened by the details of the project. It's important to remember that any change in practice or process changes the work and work experience of someone in the organization. Be aware of who will be affected by the shifts and ensure that they are informed and invited into the process to speak from experience and offer suggestions for dealing with necessary changes. As we've said before, risk awareness is everybody's business.

At this point, be sure that you have identified a project manager and ERM team, an easy to understand description of the purpose, goals, activities and timeline for your ERM planning effort If you're using the app, you can enter this information in the project overview text box as illustrated in Figure 4.3.

It is important to remember that risks arise all the time and are often unpredictable by nature. You want to build an ERM plan that takes into account known risks that need mitigation and hypotheticals, also called scenario risks, that are based on a future state or uncertainty. You don't want to create an ERM plan that locks your organization into a set of risk mitigation activities that cannot not accommodate to the changing circumstances of nonprofit organizational life, the environment you work in, or the work you do.

When you are ready, it's time to move on to the next phase: risk identification and assessment.

Risk Identification and Assessment

Now it's time to move on to identifying and assessing your priority risks. You can start with your top ten risks or use the sample list of risks as described in Chapter 2 and add organization-specific risks as you go, Once you have your risk list, drop it into the risk register and begin to dig deeper into the cause, location, severity and likelihood of each risk. Figure 4.5 shows the roadmap for risk identification and assessment.

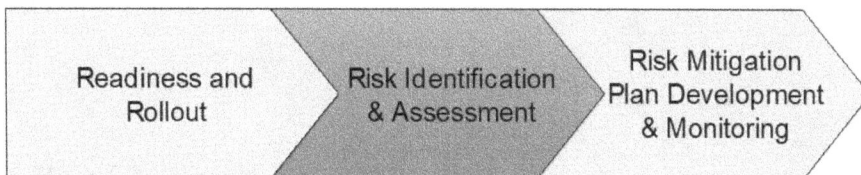

Figure 4.5: Risk Identification and Assessment

Figures 4.6 and 4.7 show the beginning of the risk identification and assessment process. On paper, we show a single form for both; with the app, the data is entered separately for the register and list. This reflects the difference between the app and paper-based interfaces. Choose whichever way is easiest for your organization.

Building the Risk List

Use the steps outlined in Chapter 2 to develop your list of risks. Again, you can start from the list of common nonprofit risks, from a risk identification session with staff, from a list developed by department and program or with the assistance of a consultant or business advisor or from your top ten risk list. As part of the assessment phase, you can highlight certain risks based on any criteria (including what resources are available to work on them), and you can prioritize them.

If you are working on paper, enter the list on a form such as the one you see in Figure 4.6. You can download it as a PDF file (see the Introduction for details). Note that the paper form combines the risk list and risk register, which you can fill in two steps.

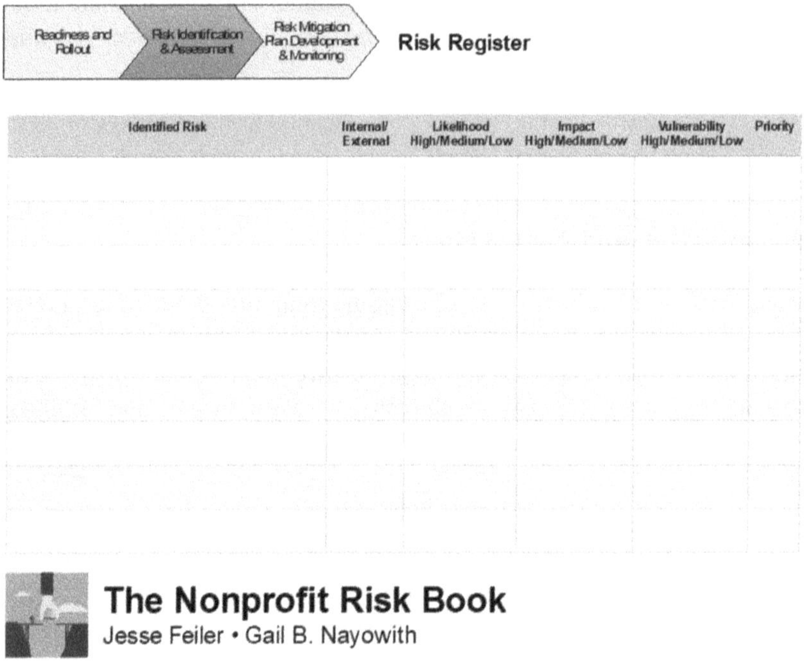
Readiness and Rollout
Risk Identification & Assessment
Risk Mitigation Plan Development & Monitoring
Risk Register

Identified Risk	Internal/ External	Likelihood High/Medium/Low	Impact High/Medium/Low	Vulnerability High/Medium/Low	Priority

The Nonprofit Risk Book
Jesse Feiler • Gail B. Nayowith

Figure 4.6: Start Your Risk List and Register in a Paper Version

If you are using the app, you generally switch back and forth between the list of risks shown in Figure 4.7 and the details for each risk shown in Figure 4.8.

| Carrier 📶 | 9:23 AM | 🔋 |
| ⓘ | **Risks** | ＋   Edit |

How Do I Start? ›

Incomplete/inaccurate Information On Activit... ›

Irregular Or Missed Board Meetings ›

Lack Of Conflict Of Interest Training ›

Long-standing Board Vacancies ›

Missing Or Outdated Mission, Staffing/Volun... ›

Noncompliance With Tax, Charity Bureau, Or... ›

Personal Use Of Petty Cash ›

Poor Accounting Practices And Financial Rev... ›

Theft Or Loss Of Physical Assets ›

Unauthorized Use Of Organization Name An... ›

Use Of Restricted Funds For A Different Pur... ›

Projects   Overview   Risk List   Risk Register   More

Figure 4.7: Enter Risks in a List in the App

Tap Edit to enable the + button and add new risks. When you're done, tap Done which replaces the Edit button or Cancel which will appear at the left. As is the case with all lists in the app, tap the disclosure button at the right of each item in the list to add its details. Figure 4.8 shows the details entry view for a risk.

The details for each risk shown in Figure 4.8 may give you pause. You will need to consider which programs or departments may be home to the risk, which activities in the program or department may be causing or interacting in a way to cause risk and whether the program or department has the capacity to resolve the identified risk. You may check and uncheck the checkboxes a number of times as you delve into the causes and possible mitigation strategies. Filling in the details for each risk as shown in Figure 4.8 is a critical part of the process.

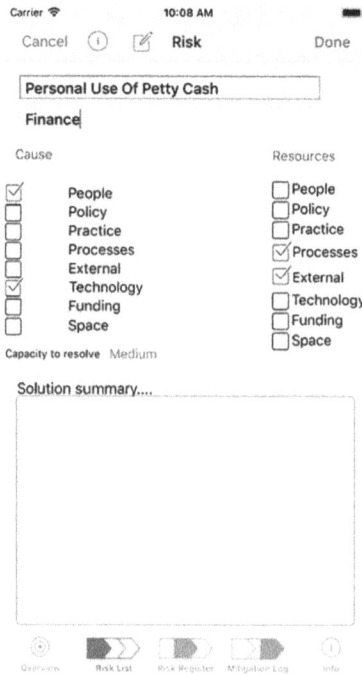

Figure 4.8: Provide Details for Each Risk.

Note: Figure 4.8 shows aspects of your organization. They may correspond to some or all of the functional areas discussed in Part II, but often they are different.

Turning the Risk List into a Risk Register

If you are working with paper, such as the downloadable PDF files, move the data from your risk list into the risk register shown previously in Figure 4.6.

With the app, your risk register is already populated with your risk list when you tap the Risk Register tab as you see in Figure 4.9.

The controls at the top of the window let you sort the risk register. As you see in Figure 4.8, that is the same data you have in columns on paper as seen in Figure 4.6.

What matters is that you have the information available in whatever format you are comfortable with. Make sure that there are no omissions.

For each risk in the risk register, add its details using the disclosure triangle at the right of the risk in the risk register. Figure 4.10 shows the details for a risk register item.

Figure 4.9: Turn Your Risk List into a Risk Register

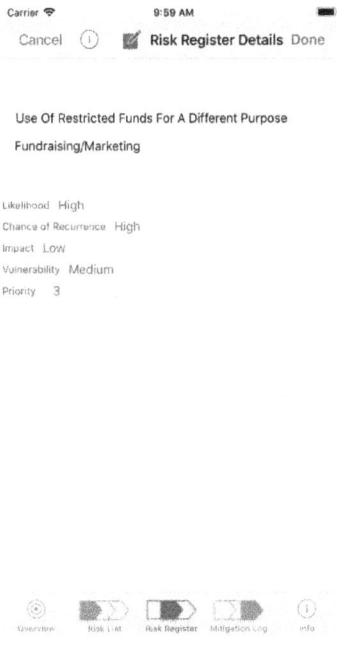

Figure 4.10: Add Details for a Risk Register Item with the App

Note: It is expected that your assumptions may change as you work with the data and look at it in various ways, sort it, and review it. Understanding the data and what it reflects about your organization is a normal part of the process that will help you identify and assess risks.

Risk Mitigation Plan Development & Monitoring

With your risk register in hand, you can move on to a risk mitigation plan as seen in Figure 4.11.

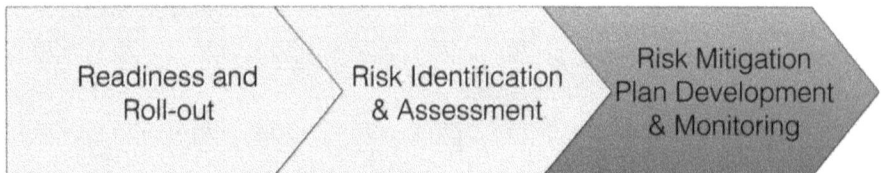

Figure 4.11: Moving on to Mitigation

After completing your risk register, you can create a mitigation log that captures the activities you will undertake to reduce organizational risks. For each risk, you now need to develop mitigation actions. Again, you can do this on paper or with the app. With the app, your mitigation log starts from your risks, as seen in Figure 4.12.

You can add more actions to each identified risk, and you can sort the mitigation log by the dates for creating, reviewing, or closing each mitigation action. As with the risk register, the more ways you rearrange the data and work with it, the more you will understand your organization and its risks.

You can add new mitigation actions for each risk by tapping on Edit and then + as you see in Figure 4.12. Once you have created a new mitigation action, tap the disclosure triangle at the right of a mitigation action to provide its details as you see in Figure 4.13.

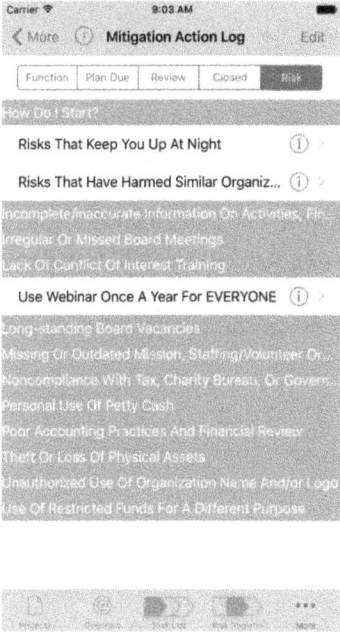

Figure 4.12: Starting to Build the Risk Register in the App

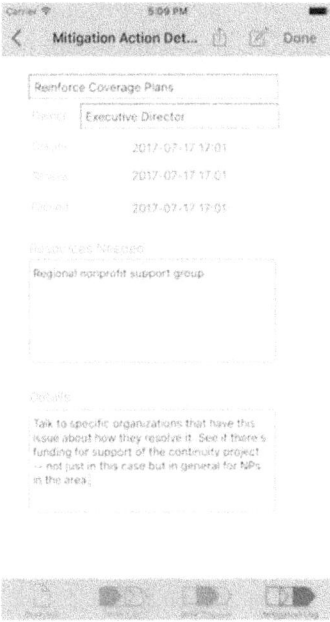

Figure 4.13: Adding Details for Mitigation Action in the Mitigation Log

Summary

In this part of the book, we recapped the enterprise risk management process starting from preparation for ERM, continuing to risk identification and assessment, and moving to mitigation planning for an ERM plan you developed for your own organization. In the second part of the book, we will explore risk in the functional areas of nonprofit operations and offer practical insights to deepen risk awareness and inspire creative solutions. You'll see what they are, what general warning signs you should watch for, and specific questions to ask to identify and understand the risks. Only by understanding the risks can you develop a meaningful and successful mitigation plan.

Part II: **Nonprofit Operating Risk**

Chapter 5
Programs & Services

For most people, a nonprofit is what it does. The programming offered and services delivered are the public-facing front door to any nonprofit organization. A nonprofit's programming appears as the most visible aspect of its operations. It's what the community, donors and government see first and it's the place where some of the biggest organizational challenges lie so it's an obvious place to look when starting your risk assessment and management work. Risk also occurs in other departments and functions such as finance, communications, personnel and governance. We will cover each in turn in this section of *The Nonprofit Risk Book*.

The activities described in this chapter on Programs and Services include some of the most common risks for nonprofit organizations. It is important to note that while program and service risks, along with risks in governance, financial management, and staffing/human resources are the functional areas of nonprofit operations that are most commonly associated with risk, they are not the only ones to carry risk. In fact, if you look at widely publicized failures in nonprofit organizations, you will find that the cause of the closure, defunding, or leadership change were not risks that originated in programs and services at all; rather, they took root in business processes and practices and rippled out from other core functions in the organization.

The Nonprofit Risk Book describes the core business features of an organization as functional areas. The taxonomy used in the book includes eight functional areas: services, staffing, financial management, operations, fundraising, communications, governance and environment. Within the framework of functional areas of operations, we discuss specific activities and their associated risks. This is a conceptual framework to help focus thinking on risk—remembering that risk can occur in any or all organizational functions offers a way of thinking about risk and the many places where risk may occur in your organization. The functional areas covered in the second half of the book offer colorful illustrations of situations, conditions, or incidents that have occurred in organizations we know. While the particulars may either resonate or seem unfamiliar to you, we hope they offer a window into risk identification and mitigation planning. The idea is to spark your thinking and offer framing examples that may be useful in practice.

DOI 10.1515/9781501505942-005

Operational Activities and Business Functions

As we pointed out at the beginning of the book, a nonprofit organization can be viewed in terms of the various functions it performs to animate its mission. Some organizational functions are performed by specific teams or departments within the organization, while others may be outsourced to other organizations or firms. We discuss functions rather than management structure because organizational hierarchy and architecture vary widely from organization to organization whereas the core functions of a nonprofit organization take place and can be found in almost every nonprofit organization and NGO.

We look at program-related risk activities that can put organizations at risk in this chapter:

– *Focusing on Mission.* It's very easy for the organization's chartered mission to be sidetracked as funding opportunities emerge and as programs evolve.
– *Providing Programming and Services.* This is the core of the chapter and the heart and soul of nonprofit organizations.
– *Serving the Public: Patrons, Audiences, and Clients.* Dissatisfied users or customers present unique risks.
– *Collaboration, Affiliation, and Working with Other Organizations.* Few organizations can do everything on their own. Impact is often greater when organizations work together for a common cause, but collaboration carries its own risks.
– *Planning for Sustainability, Growth, and the Future.* Things always change, and a focus on how an organization will handle change or find opportunity in changes is one of the hallmarks of a nonprofit organization prepared for potential risks.

Focusing on Mission

All organizations have to focus on basic mission. For commercial organizations, this mission is generally centered on building value (often future value) or income (generally present value) for the organization's shareholders. Focusing on a mission for a commercial organization is often part of its branding and its priorities are expected to change so long as it continues to produce value. For a nonprofit organization, the mission is enshrined in organizational documents, its culture and practices, and in the menu of services and programs it offers. A nonprofit's mission is not about making money—its value is measured not in profit, but in its ability to produce a desired outcome and impact the people and community it serves.

Beyond that, the mission of a nonprofit organization is linked to its tax-exempt status, its funding, and other binding commitments. Deviation from mission can have serious financial repercussions. For a commercial organization, deviating from or changing its mission is more likely to be a matter between the organization and its customers, shareholders, and staff rather than a public matter.

Note: This is a very abbreviated discussion of the mission issues for both commercial and nonprofit organizations. For more information, consult the Charities Bureau in your state or region, the National Council of Nonprofits, or a legal advisor.

What to Watch For

One common risk for nonprofit organizations arises from their very status as nonprofits. The board members, directors, staff, clients, and public at large view the nonprofit as an organization dedicated to providing a public good rather than as an organization dedicated to a specific mission for the public good. One way in which this issue has arisen is in regard to real estate - historic buildings that are donated, owned or used under long-term leases. Take for example a stately home that has been left as a bequest to a local health clinic. The organization has been given an asset that forces it to confront the tension between the upkeep and maintenance needs of a century-old building, and its mission to providing health care to the community.

Bequests that establish organizations or that provide gifts to them often become entangled with the desire to preserve a historic structure that the organization owns. Can you run a modern health care clinic out of what was a merchant's house from over a century ago? If the establishment or bequest results in the organization and its board being forced to manage a dual mission of real estate management and historic preservation and providing health care, then the board must consider the risks of the organization spreading itself too thin and make decisions that may be painful or controversial.

Frequently, the bequest or other funding is directed to the activity, such as health care, and the physical facility is provided to help advance that activity. One risk nonprofit organizations can face is their staff and connections having multiple community interests (such as healthcare and historic preservation), but unless all interests are balanced in the organizing documents, there may not be an easy answer to these challenges. Commercial organizations have it easier because they tend not to have missions in the same sense that nonprofit organizations do. (The issue does arise for commercial organizations, but it often has to do with zoning and land-use issues in conflict with activities, rather than a governing structure of the organization.)

Other areas to consider:
- Do you regularly review and revisit your organization's mission and programming for alignment to see whether it reflects changes in the community served and from which it recruits staff and board?
- Does the wording of your mission statement reflect ideas and vocabulary that identify it as old school or no longer relevant? Conversely, is your mission focused on a future that does not yet exist and is hard to imagine?

Prevention

The most basic way of preventing mission-focused risks is to ensure that everyone—including the board, director, staff, and the public—understands the mission. Understanding the mission involves not only its focus and definition, but also how the organization's mission and role differs from missions of other nonprofit, government and commercial organizations.

A second form of prevention is to establish an inventory of the governing documents, including procedures and bylaws as well as terms of gifts and bequests, to make sure they are understood. In the case of certain constraints, it may be appropriate to begin to take steps to make changes. For example, a cultural nonprofit formed by actors or musicians may, over time, evolve into an organization run by members of the public or fans of actors or musicians. This may happen without modifying the governing documents, which, nevertheless, may have strong legal force behind them.

Other issues to be reviewed are board membership constraints, in more general terms. For older institutions, there may be restrictions on residency, age, gender, or other characteristics of board members, which may need to be updated. At the same time, as this project goes on, you may also want to review general bylaws to see if they need modernization.

Mitigation

Note: Mitigation for an activity as a whole is not always possible or even necessary. However, you need to mitigate as much of the problem anywhere in the activity, just as you would any other general risk event. Where specific mitigation actions are available for an activity, they are listed in this book.

In an ideal world, your prevention efforts eliminate the need for mitigation, but we don't live in that world. In the case of mission focus, this is particularly difficult because identifying inconsistencies between the founding legal focus of an organization and its current practice may uncover issues to be resolved, which may take time. Should such an issue be uncovered, make certain that there is a plan in place to resolve it in some way so that it doesn't suddenly become front-page news.

As is often the case, deciding to keep something private—particularly in the nonprofit world—can just make things worse.

Providing Programming & Services

With the focus on the mission secure, you can turn your attention to the actual programming and services that your organization provides. Although the range of programming and services in nonprofit organizations is vast—from providing housing for the homeless to libraries, operas, and museums to the public—the risks involved in providing these services often have remarkable similarities.

What to Watch For

The basics of providing services are the same for commercial, government, and nonprofit organizations. Presumably, you have the basic best practices in place for your type of programming and services, including making certain that the offerings are consistent with the demand and that they are effective. Periodic reviews and surveys of both participants and non-participants, be they patients, customers, attendees, or staff, can help the organization know whether it is on the right track. Legal and grant-related recordkeeping is only a part of the data you need to collect. A one-time consultation (and subsequent action) based on modern principles of data science, statistics, and business analytics—somewhat overlapping terms for the basic concept—can help you understand the data that you need to collect and how to make it as useful and actionable as possible.

For most nonprofits, a key program metric is attendance and use of your offerings. In this case, you should be carefully maintaining records of use. You also should have records pertaining to the details of an event or use, including date, time, location, comments from participants, media reviews and articles, and records of providers and leaders.

The absence of attendance and vacancy data or records is a clear warning sign that there are likely other significant gaps in program operations or quality.

Here are some other areas to consider.

– Do you solicit feedback annually from users and attendees on their experiences, as well as non-users and non-attendees to understand why they don't take advantage of these opportunities?
– Do you track media comments —including social media—coverage of your organization? This can include critical and inaccurate media coverage and negative stories, which can sully your reputation with clients, participants, and donors.
– Are your programs and services fully subscribed, or do you have no-shows, vacancies, or long waiting lists?

Prevention

An important prevention action for programming and services risks involves data collection. For all events and services, you should have a standard procedure to capture the details of the event in a database or spreadsheet. Management (board and staff) should agree on the data and protocols for its collection, storage, and retention. If you do not have these policies in place, it may take time to structure them. Depending on your organization, it may be worthwhile starting with the most obvious data and gradually refining it. The alternative—waiting until everything is "right"—may end up taking so much time that it never happens. Although the details differ by organization and type of service, the basics are:

– Type of service
– Date and time of use
– Provider/leader/talent
– Users/participants
– Revenue (both direct from fees, and from collateral sources such as food, souvenirs, and any revenue other than direct)
– Pre-, contemporaneous, and post-media reports and press releases
– Comments from users/participants, organizers, providers, and talent

You can create a spreadsheet or database with these headings. Spend some time going over it with your colleagues who may have more front-line experience than you do. Don't worry about getting the initial reporting as perfect as possible: worry about getting the idea of reporting started. You can continue to review your reporting as time goes on, but if you wait until you have the perfect reporting instrument or database, you may never start collecting the data you need.

If you capture this data in multiple formats or systems, either consolidate the data or provide clear standards for sharing it. The data should be immediately available—if it takes two weeks to collect it from multiple spreadsheets and databases, it will be less useful.

Depending on your events and services, make sure you also keep track of important things that *don't* happen, such as:

– No-shows
– Empty seats/slots/space
– Speaker/trainer/talent no-show, late arrival/departure

For services that are offered or provided over a period of time, you may need to keep track of no-shows and excess capacity on a weekly or location basis.

As you collect data on programming and services, make certain that your collection and maintenance procedures respect the privacy of individuals and the laws that govern your organization and its data. The balance that you strike may need a robust mechanism for allowing people to opt out of data collection, as well as the anonymization of personally identifiable information if laws, best practices, and your own policies permit that.

Perhaps the biggest risk involving programming and services is the risk that all organizations take in providing programming and services. Everything from snowstorms and hurricanes to transportation disruptions and parades can interrupt programming and services. The fact that you cannot control these external risks doesn't mean that you shouldn't plan for them. Memory is a remarkable thing. We don't often remember common things, but we do remember the exceptions (the hurricanes, the standing-room only crowd, and the like). Keeping track of utilization and incidents that interrupt attendance can help you to see how common these special events really are.

There are some areas that you should focus on that generally do not affect other types of organizations. Because nonprofit organizations often play a public role, you may be expected or required to provide programming and services whether they are used or not and whether they are funded or not. Reviewing the requirements to which you are subject and staying on top of changes that may affect the scope of your services is essential.

Serving the Public: Patrons, Audiences, and Clients

The people and communities that you serve are a key part of your organization's structure and operations. They bring with them a variety of risks that you must prepare to handle.

What to Watch For

An organization that serves the public in any way has a variety of challenges to watch out for. Identifying the target population you serve helps to pinpoint the specific risks involved in doing so. Presumably, you know the public(s) that you serve, including their needs and characteristics. If your facilities and programming don't meet user expectations, you will encounter problems with attendance, staff turnover, underused facilities. There are risks involved in mismatches, and they are particularly likely as there are changes either to the population served, the services provided, or the facilities.

Prevention

The larger and more diverse the public that you serve, the more opportunities there are for risks. Here are some of the risk challenges to watch for.

- Changes to your public, facilities or services can throw a well-balanced and organized operation off-kilter. Whenever changes occur, be certain that you review all patron or client-facing activities of the organization that are relevant to the public being served. In particular, watch out for the less visible parts of the organization. For example, an annual book discussion group in a library may rely on a meeting space that is quiet and accessible without steps, even though it is a once-yearly event that serves only a handful of people.
- When you are serving the public, you often are also dealing with other organizations and people, many of whom you do not control or serve directly. Keeping track of how the public, including those who are not currently members perceive your organization and its operations is essential, particularly in the age of social media.
- Be certain that you and the members of the public understand which parts of your interactions are confidential (sharing personal information or use of credit cards) and ensure that this confidentiality is enforced and data security rules are followed.
- Perhaps it is just an aspect of today's world, or maybe it is more common in non-profit organizations, but be aware that you may be interacting with members of the public who also play other roles within your organization. Board members may also be audience members or users of your other services, and, in fact, many consider it part of their responsibility to use your services. Ensuring that everyone has a clear understanding of which role a person is serving in at a given moment helps avoid conflicts.
- Depending on the organization, you may need formal terms of service and responsibility for the organization and the public.

Some questions to consider include:
- Do program staff members have the expertise needed to perform well?
- Do we review a set of criteria before applying for grants or opening new programs?
- Is our staff comfortable using our data management and reporting systems that track client information, services provided, outcomes, and that generates reports?
- Do all staff members receive required program and compliance training, regular supervision, and refreshers?
- Are all programs properly staffed and are there sufficient staff to meet the needs of the community served?
- Do we review activity, quality, performance, and outcome data regularly?
- Are all of our programs appropriately subscribed and all slots, seats, and beds filled?
- Is our staff vacancy and turnover rate comparable to other organizations doing similar work?
- Do we review incidents, quality, and performance monthly and develop remediation plans to correct issues that emerge?

Working with Other Organizations

Some nonprofit organizations are totally self-contained: they carry out their activities with their own resources (think of a basic science research facility). Others have greater or lesser degrees of public engagement and engagement with other nonprofit, commercial, and governmental organizations. In many cases, a collaborative project among multiple organizations is an effective and often necessary way of meeting a community need.

What to Watch For

One of the biggest risk areas occurs when a nonprofit works with a new partner organization for the first time. Affiliations, alliances, and partnerships take a bit of calibration on both sides to make them work properly and there are many places where risks emerge and lead to failure in communications or coordination or accountability.

Another area of risk is when the two organizations are distinctly different sizes and use different management structures. In other words, operational or organization differences among partners may also be a source of risk.

Here are some other areas to consider.
- Do program staff members from partner organizations have the expertise and training needed to perform well together?
- Are the two organizations' staff vacancy and turnover rates comparable? As previously noted, this is a matter that should concern your own organization, but for collaborative endeavors, you should consider it in the context of two or more organizations individually and together.

Prevention

These are some practices to consider to prevent known risks.
- Make certain that there is clear, accurate, and timely communication about joint issues.
- Identify any differences in operations and policies that may come into play. These range from terms of payment and reimbursement (particularly paperwork, computer systems, and scheduling), to insurance covering people and facilities in joint ventures, to documenting differences and procedures for cooperation.
- Be sure that there are clear responsibilities for unexpected contingencies.
- Clarify who speaks for the project—whether it is one of the organizations or a joint responsibility.

- In any plans for joint responsibilities and operations, consider that they may need to be exercised quickly as unexpected issues arise.
- Plan from the start for termination and separation of the organizations.
- Don't assume that data and data systems can integrate easily whether they are based on the same technologies or not.

Mitigation

If there are issues related to a joint venture, here are some of the mitigation strategies that may be useful.

- Have an incident reporting and communication process in place. Before multiple versions arise about what has happened, be certain that there is a single statement of events.
- Formalize and document communication and commitments. Reduce risk by keeping records and producing tracking reports.

Planning for Sustainability, Resizing, and the Future

It is not enough to plan for the present; every organization needs to plan for its future.

What to Watch For

In addition to the planning issues faced by all organizations, nonprofits deal with an additional set of unique challenges. Among issues to watch for are governance issues. In many ways, these are similar to governance issues of privately held businesses. The "founderitis" issue, in which either a founder or the initial founders of an organization have trouble actually leaving or passing the torch to their successors, is a common risk in nonprofits and should be anticipated and watched. Managing the transition to a second generation of management (either in terms of age or point of view) is a challenge many organizations face.

Likewise, long-term planning is not unique to nonprofits, but that planning often needs to include planning and multiple scenarios for the future of supporting organizations and client organizations. For example, many long-established cultural organizations today are confronting issues of an aging base of benefactors, audiences, clients, and workers and reduced funding and support from government.

Among the changes you can expect to encounter, remember that personnel matters will loom large. For many nonprofits the bulk of their spending is on personnel. Over time, some organizations founded by volunteers have become professionally staffed organizations. Credentials and salaries for employees may change to such an extent that staff or board may express the sentiment that "the soul of the organization" has been lost. Transitions of this kind and in fact transitions of any kind whether in leadership, branching out to new communities, adding new programs or changing recipient populations increase the potential for risk that can delay or divert attention from your new goals.

Prevention

These are some steps to take when planning for the future.

Scan the field to learn about new priorities or directional shifts by other nonprofit organizations, not just for guidance in scenario planning but for an indication of where your field may be headed. Use these observations to consider how your organization may have to adapt to fit into a changed environment.

Resizing means planning not only for growth but also for consolidation as well as restructuring. Making certain you stay true to mission and understand the difference between what your organization does and how it does it will avoid risk.

Look at sustainability not just in the environmental sense, but also in the sense of how your organization will change and thrive in the future. Libraries must plan for changes in a world of eBooks, and the changing services patrons expect.

- Sustainability also means considering what to do when an organization's goals are achieved either through the organization's efforts or through external actions. Life spans are increasing and many elderly people prefer to live at home. Long term care facilities need to consider the changing preferences of clients and their families.
- When it comes to societal changes (eBooks, social media, changing political priorities, and the like), have enough discussion at the C-level (the chief executive and other chief positions) and board to be able to decide in general and specific instances if you want to be a leader (early adopter), a laggard ("old fashioned", perhaps), or in between. The organization's culture plays an outsized role in accepting and adopting news ways of working. It is also a place where risk can live or be addressed. In addition, remember that an overall organizational approach to change often is complex. In certain areas, the appetite for change is much greater than in other areas of the organization.
- Don't assume that everyone will appreciate every good thing you do. You should be proactive and pointing to the good work you do and prepared to acknowledge missteps soon after they occur. A communications plan and crisis communications apparatus should be an ongoing part of your overall social media, outreach and engagement and media monitoring activities. It is harder to disparage an organization that has documented, validated and communicated its good deeds and mistakes made through ratings, testimonials and satisfied service recipients.

Mitigation

If you encounter a risk event in this activity, as is the case with many of the events in this book, mitigate the adverse effects by following the preventive steps you've already taken. Even so, these issues need to be addressed.

- Try to anticipate and assess the impact of change in your programs and services as early and often as possible. An expected negative reaction and or cataclysmic threats often turn out to be less extreme in reality. Rather than deal with the generality of changes, examine the specific impacts that happen and may affect your organization.
- To mitigate the fallout from "soul of the organization lost" perceptions, look to any other type of organization in your field (not just nonprofits). These changes can have long-term and deep-seated consequences.
- Don't assume that the world and your followers are watching and appreciating every good thing you do. You should be proactive and point to the good work you do and it should be an ongoing part of your social media campaign. It is harder to attack an organization that has created a verified wall of good deeds that can be enhanced by quotes, testimonials and so on.

Summary

As the most visible part of your organization, programming and services is an area where risks cluster and where one incident can turn into a crisis. In this chapter you see things to watch out for and steps to take to mitigation and manage problems.

Several steps to take to prevent problems recur in various contexts (not only in this chapter but throughout the book). Keep track of what happens (and doesn't happen) in a convenient and systematic way; relying on memory is a poor substitute for contemporaneous documentation.

Watch and listen to what happens and how your programming and services are received in the community. Make certain that you don't bias or prejudice your collection of comments about your work: search out general reactions as well as specifically searching for positive and negative responses.

In many ways, the programming and services your organization provides is all that people know about your organization.

Chapter 6
Personnel

If you compare nonprofit organizations with commercial and governmental counterparts, among the biggest differences is the central role played by boards and volunteers. Nonprofit organizations rely on board members and volunteers who offer uncompensated assistance and pro bono service alongside paid staff.

Human resources—talent and staffing—are key to nonprofit success because all activities are completed by, with, and through people. In nonprofit organizations typically upwards of 80% of the organization's budget is spent on staffing or volunteer supports. Staffing and talent management is an area of significant risk for most nonprofits. We focus on some key personnel risks for nonprofit organizations.

As we have worked on this book, friends and colleagues have shared stories with us, and many of them have to do with personnel. Perhaps that's because many of the personnel anecdotes are among the most colorful and easy to understand examples of nonprofit risk. In and of itself, that is one of the biggest risks organizations face: the personnel stories are so easy to understand and, in many cases, so outrageous, that they make great material for news articles and exposés. The raw material is terrific from an editor's point of view. The story can have everything—a story that's easy to tell, often a big financial loss, and, on top of that, a relatively easy to find story of the innocent people who have been hurt by incompetence, criminal intent, lax supervision, or some combination of these. We have tried to share with you some of the real-life adventures we have seen and heard in the nonprofit world, but it is in the area of personnel, that we have put several of those stories aside because we fear no one would believe them.

The risks described in this chapter are:
- Working for good
- Conflicts of interest
- Conflicts of role
- Managing credentials and performance appraisals
- Working with management
- Reliance on volunteers to deliver service or hold client/community facing positions
- Compensation ceilings on executive pay

Working for Good

The ethos undergirding work in the nonprofit and NGO sector can be characterized by the phrase, "working for good." The assumption is that working for good is distinct from working for profit.

DOI 10.1515/9781501505942-06

There is often a disparity in pay between nonprofits and their government and commercial counterparts. The disparities vary from organization to organization and from field to field. But typically, staff in nonprofit organizations come to work on mission, doing good, or making the world a better place.

The topic of pay discrepancies between nonprofits, government and commercial enterprises is worth thinking about because it is part of the nonprofit and NGO landscape and directly affects recruitment, retention and turnover of staff. In and of itself, it doesn't always create risk, but it does drive organizational culture and the risk and reward atmosphere in and around the organization.

Personnel in Action

Personnel risks occur in every functional area of operations. Not all staffing risks are unique to nonprofit organizations.

What to Watch For

Here are some of the most common risk factors in personnel activities for nonprofits.

- When there is a mix of paid staff and volunteers, is it clear what standards and rules apply to each group? For example, rules about the amount of time off allowed may differ for the two groups, but it is perfectly reasonable to have common standards regarding notices given for planned absences.
- Employees of nonprofits often know what is happening in their field whether their comparisons are with commercial or nonprofit organizations. Not only can they compare salaries and benefits, but they can compare opportunities for training. With constrained budgets, some organizations (both commercial and nonprofit) sometimes "economize" by minimizing out-of-office training. In both commercial and for-profit organizations, this can often be a false economy. In some environments, nonprofits are more competitive in terms of training and professional development, which can help counteract lower salaries. In other environments, the reverse is true.
- In using volunteers for any purpose, does the organization have a policy and practice of thanking and celebrating volunteers for their service? Volunteer work is valuable both to the organization and the volunteers, and should be recognized as such.

Additionally, the following risk factors also need to be identified.

- Do personnel, including managers, clearly understand their roles and responsibilities as well as those of the organization itself?

- Do all personnel (volunteers and paid) have the skills, training, and regular supervision they need to do their jobs? If they are routinely asked to perform other tasks, is there a clear protocol for managing those requests? Is there a protocol for passing on the information so that training or resources can be provided next time the situation arises?
- Is there a convenient and useful method of tracking services provided by volunteers and converting this in-kind assistance to a revenue projection? "Useful" means that is useful to staff, managers, and those members of the public who need access to it.
- For activities that involve standards and compliance, are employee and volunteer policies and handbooks updated annually to reflect changes in legislation or regulations? Are your pre-service, in-service, and compliance refresher trainings updated regularly to conform to new requirements or organizational needs? (This can apply to volunteers and paid staff.)
- Do you track and understand the root causes of staff and volunteer vacancies and turnover? Are your vacancy and turnover rates comparable to peer organizations?
- Do staff and volunteers have access to the technology they need to do their work and clear rules about the proper way to handle information? This is particularly important so that confidential data about the organization and the people it serves is not revealed through personal email accounts, is not retained on personal devices, or otherwise shared without permission.
- Are there clearly understood guidelines for the use of social media?

Conflicts of Interest

Conflicts of interest appear in all organizations. A conflict of interest arises when a staff member, board member or volunteer has an interest in or stands to profit from a transaction or decision made by the organization. That is why nonprofits need a conflict of interest policy and regular training for staff, board members and volunteers. Conflict of interest policies protect the nonprofit organization's interests particularly when it is contemplating a transaction that could benefit the private interest of an officer or director or staff person or related party.

What to Watch For

Here are several examples of conflicts of interest and how they may arise.
- *Independence of board members.* Members of a nonprofit board are assumed to be independent and objective people who are interested in the organization and its activities, and who will work to advance and promote the goals of the organization as their primary concern when they are serving on the board. A healthy

nonprofit board has a diversity of people with relevant expertise and perspectives. Particularly in small communities, conflicts can abound. For example, in a board of five members, if two are closely related, it is necessary to guard against the appearance that they may be acting together to further personal interests, which may not be totally congruent with those of the organization.

– *Financial interests of board members.* If a nonprofit board is considering hiring a contractor for a roofing project and a board member owns a firm that will bid on the work, the organization's conflict of interest policy should serve as a protection against the appearance of self-dealing or financial gain. Provisions in the policy for disclosure and recusal can offer nonprofit organizations the opportunity to consider such a bid while protecting the organization's interests and resources. These situations pose many risks as does a situation where a board member or relative offers to do the work at a reduced price that benefits the business as well as the organization.

– *Conflicts of interest with staff and clients.* Conflict of interest policies also offer protection against reputational risk. Strong policies and annual training can prevent accusations that a board member or staff person has given favorable treatment based on a personal relationship or financial interest.

Prevention

It is considered an essential practice for members of a nonprofit board and executive staff to review the organization's conflicts of interest policy annually. Minutes that include board action to approve the updated policy and signed attestations that board members have received training are best practice. Some key elements of the policy should include:

– The board member's or staff person's name and the date.
– The board member's or staff person's position (officer title, or other reference).
– An easily understandable definition of the conflict-of-interest policy for the organization and the board member's or staff person's signed acknowledgment of having reviewed the policy and an attestation of no conflict.
– In the event of a conflict, the policy provides opportunity for disclosure and notification to the executive director, board chair, or board committee, and for recusal on the matter.

Many organizations provide their boards with a list of businesses with which they deal. Board member attestations can indicate if they have any financial stake, business, or personal interest in those organizations.

In this type of situation, it is up to individual board members to disclose potential conflicts of interest. The policy describes the process for handling the matter without the board member present. It is the board's decision or advice from counsel as to whether or not a conflict of interest exists and, if so, what steps should be taken to handle it. Typically, the step taken is to ask the board member not to participate in discussions and or decision- making that could present a conflict of interest.

Note: This is a description of how some organizations handle conflicts of interest. You should consult counsel, the relevant charities oversight organizations, as well as legislation and regulations when drafting a conflict of interest policy. Be sure that your organization's documents are reviewed annually for conformance with local requirements.

Conflicts of Role

Conflicts of role are similar to conflicts of interest, but they arise when a board member performs multiple roles that are supposed to be independent.

What to Watch For

A typical example is when a board member serves as a volunteer working for the organization in addition to that as a board member. For example, in a library, a board member may assist in shelving books or maintaining a schedule for public meeting rooms. In a community organization, a board member may help to guide walking tours or work in a food pantry operation.

All people who work for or with the organization, whether as staff, volunteers, board members, or contractors and consultants, need to identify their roles when interacting with people inside and outside of the organization. In some organizations, this is managed with ID badges of different colors or shapes, but even the smallest organization needs to identify who people are and what their roles are. Business cards are useful, but people need to know that their role is important in dealing with the public. Particularly with people who have multiple roles, it's important that they clarify the role in situations where it may matter. "I'm Jesse, a software developer," are partial identifications. Are you the chief executive, or, when you say that you're "from" an organization, are you merely describing your physical location at that moment? A software developer who is auditing operations is different from a software developer who is blind-calling a potential client to see about selling services.

Prevention

A way of preventing role conflicts is for board members who work as volunteers to make it clear to everyone that they are volunteering as a member of the public and not as a board member. Having clear policies and protocols for handling complaints and other incidents can help to avoid situations where board members are approached to deal with issues that should be handled according to the protocol.

Working with Management

Typically, an executive director is responsible for selecting the senior staff, and the board is responsible for selecting the executive director. In some cases, the board may interview and ratify appointments of senior staff that are made by the executive director. As is true in any organization, be it nonprofit, governmental, or commercial, clarifying the chain of command and the responsibilities of each participant in hiring decisions is critical to the success of the organization. One piece of advice is agreed upon: clarify these issues *before* you need to.

What to Watch For

There are times when a specific executive director has responsibilities that another executive director may not have; clarifying those circumstances is essential if the organization, its board, and its executive directors (now and in the future) are to succeed.

From time to time, people try to circumvent the clearly stated protocols that identify how to support transparency and communication as well as protecting whistleblowers by going outside the protocol.

Having clear rules, guidelines, and procedures can minimize confusion. If the guidelines are clear, it should be obvious when they are being flouted, and that in turn makes it clear to people who can identify when there is a problem.

Prevention

In addition to a clear chain of command, there needs to be a clear and promulgated chain of complaint and redress. This is required by law in some cases, where there must be alternative paths for the affected party to choose.

A common chain of complaint is that issues can move up a ladder of redress so there are multiple opportunities for resolution. They can be moved up the chain of command until they reach the executive director or board. When a board member is serving as a volunteer, people should not take that as an alternative route to conflict resolution.

In a small organization run by volunteers, the board may determine what tasks or jobs are done in what way—that is, by volunteers, employees, or contract workers. (In the case of organizations with union workers, this can be more complicated.)

Some nonprofit organizations are structured so that although many people are employed by the organization, the board itself has a single employee: the executive director. The executive director then hires and fires the others. In other cases, the board hires or at least confirms all senior people (sometimes referred to as the *C-suite*—the chief executive officer, chief technical officer, and so forth). Another structural issue is whether or not the executive director is a member of the board.

The issue of who is responsible for hiring and firing staff is a matter to discuss with your legal advisors because it can change from place to place and time to time.

Mitigation

Situations where a board and executive director or board and staff are at odds or there is role confusion or conflicts of interest pose significant risk. It is important to watch for the warning signs of discord and miscommunication and closely monitor conflicts.

Managing Credentials and Performance Appraisals

Although the executive director is in charge of the operations and staff, the board shares responsibility for many functions, including budgeting, investments, policy making, executive compensation decisions, real estate transactions, and other oversight activities. Where standards must be enforced for everything from zoning laws to financial management and employment practices, it is the board that has governance responsibility and the executive director who has management responsibility.

In order to fulfill conditions of some grants, contracts, and operating licenses, it is necessary to verify that certifications and credentials are valid and current. For performance appraisals, the standards are basically the same as in commercial organizations. Boards set executive compensation and are required to conduct an annual performance review. Some jurisdictions, like New York State, regulate the details of these processes. With nonprofits, both the credentialing process and the performance appraisals may take different forms. When volunteers are involved, standards may be different than they are for employees or consultants. It is the responsibility of the board and executive director to know what the requirements are and to ensure that the organization is in compliance.

What to Watch For

One important thing for a board to watch for in the process of managing performance appraisals is timeliness. Tracking the status of credential and appraisal dates is an expected part of board oversight. Many jurisdictions now require boards to do salary and comparability studies among peer organizations before awarding raises or bonuses to executive directors.

Significant tardiness in conducting annual appraisals can be a red flag. The best way of preventing problems is to keep appraisals up to date (and, from the beginning, having a clear schedule of expiration and renewal dates.

Tip: As in commercial organizations, it is critical to look at performance appraisals as basic management tools that can be of use to everyone. Smart nonprofits provide annual performance reviews for all staff and volunteers. This provides an opportunity for professional development, a rationale for any salary increase or change in duties, and a way to assess potential and fit.

Prevention

Clarity around roles and responsibilities, performance expectations and communication is a starting point in reducing risk. Specifically, make certain that the chains of command and redress are clear, job and task descriptions are up-to-date (including those for volunteers, consultants, contractors, and employees), and an ongoing schedule for appraisals is followed.

Tip: One practice from many organizations, both commercial and nonprofit, can be very useful. Make sure that performance appraisals and salary reviews occur at a fixed point in time—perhaps the employee's anniversary date, or on a fixed calendar cycle.

Summary

Personnel practices are an area of great vulnerability for nonprofit organizations. If you examine risks that have been uncovered in nonprofit organizations, you will find that many of them have a large personnel connection. You can argue about whether the problem is actually a personnel issue, one of not having appropriate protocols and procedures, a case of not following existing protocols and procedures or some combination of these and other matters, but personnel activities loom large in many known nonprofit organization risk problems.

The themes of this chapter and of effective risk avoidance are to know what is going on, to be certain that everyone knows the rules, and to be as open as possible.

Chapter 7
Environment, Regulatory, and Compliance Issues

There are many similarities and some distinct differences across types of nonprofits and nongovernmental organizations. Assuming that all nonprofits are alike when thinking about risk can have disastrous consequences. Think about the kind of knee-jerk reaction that can happen when managers or boards react to a crisis in another organization by taking a course of action or proposing a solution to a problem you don't have.

Nonprofit and non-governmental organizations are required to meet many statutory and regulatory requirements. For some activities, NPOs and NGOs are more heavily regulated than other types of organizations. This chapter explores some of these issues.

If you think that you're too small (or too new or too specialized or too anything else) to have to worry about these issues that may seem to affect only other organizations, think again. On the one hand your organization may change in many ways and may find itself —perhaps suddenly—confronting new challenges in environment and regulatory areas. On the other hand, regulations and laws may change so that organizations that are not covered by some of the regulations discussed in this chapter are covered—again, perhaps with little warning. On the positive side, there are lessons to be learned and it's good to be able to learn them before you're suddenly confronted with the need to change your practices on someone else's timetable.

Here are some activities commonly involved in environment and regulatory issues for nonprofits:
- Managing in the Community and Operating Environments
- Managing Compliance and Regulations
- Responding to Catastrophic Environmental Risks
- Being Part of the Nonprofit Environment

Managing in the Community and Operating Environments

The environment of a nonprofit organization is both the neighborhood or location in which the organization functions and the group or groups of people served or employed by the organization. The community includes staff, sponsors, funders, clients, elected officials, other organizations or users of services offered or they may also simply be neighbors. If your organization wants to close off the street for a block party, support from your community matters, especially if you need a permit or expect to use fencing or ropes that block access to their homes and businesses. Maintaining cordial relationships and being responsive to the needs of neighbors is key to reducing negative incidents and other environmental risks.

DOI 10.1515/9781501505942-007

When it comes time to apply for funding or a building permit, support from neighbors can matter as much as or more than support from clients, users, and people who are served by the organization. (In fact, in some cases, having support from people who are *not* served by your organization enhances your chances of approval.)

Organizations can be viewed as "good" or "bad" neighbors. Organizations that might be considered possible bad neighbors need to make special effort to support neighbors or neighborhood groups in order to improve their relations or get permission to locate in a neighborhood. What makes a community consider certain types of organizations bad neighbors varies greatly. In some neighborhoods, any organization whatsoever that will bring more traffic to the area or compete for scarce parking spaces might be considered "bad." Sometimes it's residential programs, sites with heavy foot traffic or late hours of operation or programs that are noisy like a youth orchestra or an opera conservatory with vocal lessons or string quartet practice studios that can cause friction with the community. This is an issue that varies by type of nonprofit and the programming offered organization as well as by the preferences of a community neighborhood. Risk comes when you don't balance organizational and community needs. Lack of sensitivity and failure to proactively build good will and good relationships create or exacerbate risk.

The operating environment for an organization also consists of the laws, rules, and regulations under which it functions. These change often and failure to stay current or update policies and procedures to reflect these changes pose risk for your organization.

The operating environment also includes fellow organizations or groups that join together to collaborate on activities, take action on shared priorities, advocate for change or against a law, regulation or budget cut (in a broader sense, any organization or body that has a stake in your organization or in which you have a stake).

What to Watch For

Don't ask if your organization scans and keeps track of changes in the operating environment: ask *how* it does that. An important board oversight activity is to make certain that the organization has a process to receive and resolve community complaints, that it acts as a good neighbor and that it scans and tracks changes in the operating environment. Board members who are also community residents, service recipients or are involved with multiple community organizations, bring special value to a nonprofit organization. Their insights and relationships can be an invaluable asset and source of information. Nonprofit executives also monitor the operating environment for change, opportunity or risk and use this information to plan ahead.

At a high level, watch for an organization that has limited or no awareness of its operating environment: that is a clear risk. There should be formal and informal processes in place that allow the executive and board to receive notice of changing statutes, regulations, competitors, and alliances.

Part of the operating environment is the community in which your organization functions. Many nonprofits have formalized the way they do community outreach and engagement. They are able to produce an annual activity report that includes targets and goals met. Risk attentive organizations do community consultations before embarking on a new service offering and they conduct community surveys or hold open houses to elicit feedback and build constructive relationships.

Prevention

Because the operating environment changes frequently, it's a good idea to identify a source that provides regular updates and a dynamic news feed, such as RSS or a blog, and social media platforms such as Facebook, Twitter, and Instagram or set up Google alerts, so that you can keep track of latest developments including discussions of pending changes or proposals under consideration.

What you want is an expert and validated information source that is easily digestible for managers who can translate it into alerts for executives, board and staff as needed. You will also want to follow community newsfeeds and blogs so your organization knows about community concerns and where you can learn about what is and is *not* happening—in other words, what neighborhood problems have been averted. This kind of scanning is useful in identifying and averting risk early.

An operations feed can be duplicated automatically to a Twitter account. Keep that feed focused and Twitter account tightly targeted to capture actional information (notifications and updates about school closings, for example) and make certain that you create or pass along only verifiable information. You can also use these information platforms or your own website or blog or social media to notify the community of organization activities, local events or to congratulate active volunteers and community residents, or solicit volunteers for a project. Community engagement is a necessary feature of nonprofit life. Well managed, it is a tremendous asset.

Here are some other prevention tips.
–   Do you hold an annual community meeting to gather feedback and celebrate the community?
–   Does the organization participate in or sponsor community events to support local interests or promote the organization and its activities? Sponsoring or co-sponsoring a "fun run" for kids or buying a table at a community event is the type of outreach that can be an effective way to build strong relationships.

- Is there a policy for responding quickly to written, verbal or online complaints from the community? Is a staff person tasked with monitoring and responding to on-line feedback or comments about your organization?
- Does the organization know and follow rules and regulations for advocacy, lobbying, and community relations with officials?
- Does the organization use a social media dashboard such as Hootsuite, Mention, Sprout Social, or Spredfast to track community news or mentions?

Managing Compliance and Regulations

Regulations and compliance cover everything from the treatment of patients in a medical facility to the placement of exit signs in a place of public assembly (or even in an office). Some nonprofits have dedicated central staff who manage compliance issues. Others handle compliance with program or department staff who are responsible for stating current and notifying the executive team when changes occur.

All nonprofits need a process for monitoring and complying with regulatory or other required changes. Failure to comply can result in loss of an operating license, steep fines, revocation of a government contract or other significant negative consequences. Compliance is never an optional activity.

What to Watch For

Compliance with government requirements requires particular vigilance and formal processes for implementing requirements and changes. It raises a red flag when compliance work for the organization is tacked on as additional work for a staff person with a host of other responsibilities. This is especially true for nonprofits where compliance activities are decentralized or where staff are stretched very thin. This is another reason for reinforcing the fact that nonprofit risk is everyone's business. Compliance requirements come with deadlines and penalties. Once a compliance problem is found or noted in an oversight review, there is likely to be significant additional corrective actionable work to be done, perhaps a fine to be paid, heightened monitoring by the oversight body and sometimes more intense reviews that follow. Noncompliance can create a cascade of issues. For example, failing to apply timely for a work permit needed to do a program facility repair or maintenance can quickly mushroom into a project that disrupts normal operations. Some compliance requirement changes may allow grandfathering in or give organizations time to transition to the new rules.

Tip: If your nonprofit organization is contemplating changes in programming, operations or mission, or if you have or are considering a merger with another organization, make certain to review compliance requirements and other mandates carefully and early in the process. A conservative approach includes review by your board and counsel and the assumption that you might be required to comply with the most stringent rules.

Prevention

Every nonprofit organization operating today should have a formal policy and processes for board, staff and volunteer compliance training on an annual basis. Any number of costly and disruptive penalties can come to nonprofits who don't keep track of certification or recertification deadlines. One of the best ways to keep compliance current is for managers and board managers to take it seriously. When the tone and expectations are set at the top and when compliance activities are formalized, the organization's risk exposure is reduced.

Here are some other issues to consider.
- Do you have a routinized protocol for reviewing compliance activities and updating policies to align with new compliance requirements? If staff needs guidance or the board requests information on compliance activities, is your organization prepared to provide them with a written document?
- Do you have a database or use a spreadsheet to track compliance deadlines, completed activities or progress made on corrective actions including updates needed, ratings (positive or negative) from external oversight entities of your compliance status?
- Do you conduct quarterly and annual reviews with managers to monitor completion and produce a dashboard or report to the board on the organization's compliance status and vulnerabilities?

Responding to Catastrophic Environmental Risk

All organizations need to be prepared for the possibility of floods, fires, extreme weather and other natural disasters. Emergency preparedness has also grown in scope to include safety and security, active shooter policies and protections against other acts of man. Detailed disaster plans, drills and testing have become an essential part of nonprofit risk management. Environmental risk today is defined more broadly and requires more insurance coverage and planning than in the past.

"Catastrophe" is a word that is often used when describing extreme environmental risks. External conditions are causing nonprofits to think more planfully about catastrophic events that cause loss of life, property damage and service interruption or that require storage of food, water, medical supplies and back-up generators. We use "catastrophic" in a very specific way to describe a single event or linked chain of events that threaten lives and essential operations.

The simultaneous unavailability of power, communication, and transportation over a wide geographic area means that many backup protocols and procedures in place for a single nonprofit organization will not suffice. A catastrophic environmental risk is any event that puts your people and operations at risk from an internet and cell outage to a water main break in your lobby. Disaster planning is only a starting point. Staff must be trained in emergency procedures and emergency communication processes must be in place.

Many nonprofit organizations are also expected to respond to disasters. Whether it's opening a central food distribution outlet or providing shelter or medical assistance or helping relocate displaced people after a hurricane or other catastrophic event, nonprofits are often first responders and partners in recovery work. While it is impossible to forecast with certainty catastrophic damage caused by all environmental risks, it is possible to build organizational capacity to respond to emergencies.

What to Watch For

In addition to the factors you consider when assessing the likelihood that an environmental risk event will occur and affect your organization, consider the possibility that your organization may have to deploy its resources in the service of others.

- Are your evacuation, disaster and recovery procedures formalized in writing, current and tested through drills with staff and clients regularly? Do you train staff in emergency response?
- Have you done worst and best case scenario planning with senior staff and applied lessons learned to your disaster plan and preparedness activities?
- Have you worked collaboratively with local government and other organizations in crafting a community disaster response?
- Do you store or back-up vital information offsite? Do you maintain emergency supplies on site?

Being Part of the Nonprofit Environment

Nonprofit organization tax exemptions are based on an expectation of public good. These organizations may be active in a variety of areas ranging from providing food and medicine to people in need, to building and maintaining a social club. Nonprofit tax status may exempt an organization from sales or property taxes and may confer the right to give a tax deduction for qualified donations but, it doesn't provide a blanket exemption from all fees or tax look-alikes. In some jurisdictions where government budgets are tight, nonprofits can be asked to pay PILOTS: the payment of fees for government services in lieu of taxes. Nonprofits renting space may also have leases that include payment of all or a portion of the landlord's property taxes. As well, there are often referenda or legislative proposals pending locally or nationally that threaten to strip tax exemption status from nonprofit organizations—typically but not exclusively universities and hospitals. It is important to track tax obligations and filing deadlines. In the US and Canada nonprofit organizations must file annual tax statements with the federal government. Best practice includes board review of all tax documents before they are filed. These filings are public; the details can serve as a red flag for a variety of fiscal and operational improprieties.

Peer organizations are also an important part of the nonprofit operating environment. Nonprofits can have formal or informal relationships with peer organizations. The relationships can include formal collaboration on collective impact or community projects, memoranda of understanding or contracts to deliver services to the clients of another organization, provide back-office support or serve as a fiscal intermediary for a peer organization, or pay dues to a coalition or association representing multiple organizations.

Being part of a community of nonprofit organizations has many advantages but it also carries risk. It's just as important to know your partners and how they work when doing community events as it is when there are shared financial transactions, fundraising appeals or volunteer recruitment drives.

What to Watch For

Whether you look at the nonprofit environment from the vantage point of a cause or project or in the context of place, your nonprofit organization sits in an ecosystem of relationships, obligations and activities. The board and executive director are responsible for setting the parameters of staff and organization involvement with other organizations. These parameters can be formal or informal. Recipients, staff, managers, and funders compare organizations. This creates challenges in staff recruitment and retention particularly when salary scales are not comparable. When problems occur in one organization, it is an easy leap for worry to spread and implicate all organizations even when no problem has occurred. Conversely, organizations that operate without engaging peers, risk being left behind or uninformed about opportunities.

Prevention

Staff and volunteers need to know how your organization works with partners and how to represent the organization in the community or when they are working alongside partners on a joint project. They need to have guidelines for what information can be shared and which is confidential.

Note: One of the benefits of conferences is that they provide a forum for sharing techniques and strategies without worrying about confidentiality (although conferences are sometimes closed to outsiders). Look at this from the other side and make certain that there are clear protocols to be followed to get permission when someone speaks about the organization's operations at a conference. Nonprofit organizations share many attributes, problems, and solutions, but not all of them, so make certain that you know how other nonprofits function before you work with them even on a small scale.

Summary

This chapter provides an overview of rules governing the nonprofit operating environment and the community in which nonprofits operate. Nonprofits are not identical in mission or operations, even within a small region. Human services nonprofits are both similar to and different from cultural organizations such as libraries and museums. Nonprofit industry associations may function like commercial trade groups. It's important to know your community, your partners and the environment in which your organization operates.

Chapter 8
Finance

Programs and services are often the thing that comes to mind when people think about a nonprofit organization, but finance and financial operations are what they think about first when they focus specifically on nonprofit risk. It looms large for nonprofit organizations, and those risks take many forms.

This chapter looks at three major activities in the financial area of nonprofit organizations that can pose significant risks.

The risks that are described in this chapter are:
- Managing the organization's cash, investments, and financial reputation
- Accounting for grants, activities, and overhead
- Dealing with discretionary, ad hoc, and emergency projects

Managing the Organization's Cash, Investments, and Financial Reputation

This is the heart of financial operations for any organization, including a nonprofit one. The differences between nonprofit and other types of organizations are significant enough that whoever manages your financial operations (either a part-time, preferably expert, volunteer in a small organization or an in-house staff expert or team aided by outside accountants in a large organization) needs to be aware of the differences and of all the generally accepted accounting practice rules that pertain.

In the past, some nonprofits managed accounts payable and cash flow by letting vendors know that the library, hospital, museum, or other nonprofit organization was "good for it," so there shouldn't be concern if payments were late. Whether or not this was ever really true, it is certainly no longer true today. In fact, recent failures of large nonprofit organizations have made it clear that when it comes to financial stability and reliability, good deeds and good intentions are no substitute for a reliable and well managed financial operation and board oversight of financial performance and practices.

What to Watch For

A notable red flag for nonprofits is the absence of budgeted cash reserves—too many function with a minimal cushion of cash reserve operating funds. For organizations that rely on grant funding—which, in turn, relies on approvals from funders—the time it takes to process a payment or claim can be significant. Payment delays are common

DOI 10.1515/9781501505942-008

but payroll and program operating expenses happen on a fixed schedule. Many nonprofit organizations, no matter how large or small in size, operate on a shoestring and too often have to juggle or stagger vendor payments to keep the lights on. It is important to have operating policies regarding the handling of payables that have been reviewed by your board and an outside accounting professional, particularly when there are new staff or pro bono volunteers handling your bookkeeping and finances. Simply paying bills late or handling nonprofit budgeting as you do your personal budget is not a good strategy.

There are ways to mitigate cash flow and late payment problems. In addition to traditional practices, such as lines of credit, if your nonprofit organization is dependent on one or more organizations to authorize your payments, see if you can work with your funder to change the payment calendar to better align with your expense cycle. Too many nonprofits get into trouble with lines of credit, not accounting for interest or payback in current year budgets.

As an example of an administrative solution, a public library board must approve an annual budget and certain expenditures. Once approved by the library board, those same expenditures may need to be approved by the town in which the library is located. In a situation like this where the approval process is long and where payments are often delayed, some library boards pass a resolution authorizing the payment of routine bills for routine expenses. Other nonprofits make similar administrative adjustments through annual board resolutions to allow the executive to continue spending up to a set amount for a set period of time with board approval and oversight. This type of structure preserves the board's role in approving payments, but does not require a board meeting or board vote to authorize each individual payment.

Unforeseen circumstances can arise in the course of the year, and their expenses need to be covered in one way or another. The organization can prepare for contingencies with a line of credit, cash reserves and a board approved spending plan. However, beyond the immediate need to handle an emergency, each organization needs a way to do periodic reviews of emergency or unbudgeted expenses to improve planning and reduce risks. Regardless of cause, an organization needs to keep track of emergency or off-budget spending which can be costly and be a flag for risk.

Since it is now possible to file many reports and tax documents online, your policies and procedures must include rules governing access to and handing of submissions by approved staff. Modern security best practices no longer rely on a single password, so it's necessary to test periodically to be sure that security protocols, such as two-factor authorization, are being followed and can be used properly.

Prevention

It is a best practice for boards to review tax returns and financial statements before they are submitted. Every organization is different, so this practice is followed in different ways. Make certain that you have the appropriate time and skills devoted to presenting the information clearly and understanding it in detail. "That's the normal format for a balance sheet," is not explaining things clearly. Similarly, saying, "We trust our accountants," is not a review. Not understanding a financial statement is not a sign of ignorance, nonprofit financial statements are often complex. Offering an orientation to the organization's finances and financial reporting is good practice when bringing anyone on board. Providing clear explanations and welcoming questions can be part of that process. It is better to make the time to do this early on in a member's board service than to explain a deficit, lost grant or audit finding to a roomful of angry board members about why you didn't. The fact that these conversations happen repeatedly means that everyone will become more familiar with the data, which is a good thing.

- Periodically review your internal controls and procedures, particularly when there is any change in industry rules or in the people managing them. Accounting skills and experience in other organizations—particularly commercial organizations—may not be directly applicable, so make certain that your finance staff and volunteers are trained and understand where the differences are. This is not to say that nonprofit organizations can't improve practice by learning from commercial organizations, but be sure that any change in practice is appropriate in a nonprofit context.

- If your organization has cash transactions, ensure that they are properly documented, handled and controlled. Small fundraising items sold informally are often targets of opportunity in as much as they may be handled carelessly. Cash transactions are a temptation and risk regardless of situation. Many organizations prefer to accept credit cards or checks or payment through other platforms.

- Similarly, make sure that checks given to staff by hand are properly processed and entered into your accounting system. It is not uncommon for organizations to accept checks at events or community activities where there is a lot going on. All receivables, regardless of source, must be coded to the proper activity, event or program. Since event checks or cash donations warrant a thank you or receipt this can be another way to check for process gaps.

- In small organizations where a volunteer may do the bookkeeping, provide adequate training and support and regular supervision. Make certain that you know what accounting software or spreadsheets are being used and how they are secured and maintained. Establish a process for monthly review of your financial information and build in other integrity and accountability measures to prevent theft or misuse of funds or accounting errors.

Tip: If it is discovered that your spreadsheet or financial reports don't add up, consider that a warning sign that warrants immediate investigation. Adding or changing an item on your spreadsheet or in your financial software should not create a calculation error. If it does and correction requires manual intervention, the spreadsheet is not properly set up and may mask improprieties.

- Does the board set and enforce a basic level of understanding of the organization's financial structure for all board members and management staff, including subsidiaries and partners?
- Does the board review financial statements and budgets quarterly, and the US Form 990 or other tax submissions prior to filing them with the authorities?
- Do board minutes reflect regular review of the organization's financial statements and annual review of tax submissions? A Treasurer's report that does not include financial review by the board or a named board committee is a red flag.
- Is there a financial management system in place that is sized to the needs and complexity of your organization? This might be a data system, spreadsheet, or sophisticated financial management software package. Can it produce reports regularly and on demand? Is detail available for review by board, Treasurer, and executive management?
- How many times in the last year has someone (such as a member of the board, staff, or public) asked a financial question that could not be answered? This is a red flag.

Mitigation

Problems with financial management and cash flow typically need to be handled with contingency procedures and earmarked resources, so their mitigation should be built into operating budgets and reserves and operating policies as is standard accounting practice.

Accounting for Grants, Activities, and Overhead

Many nonprofit organizations have a multitude of programs, projects and are managing support from multiple funding sources. As government and foundation funders expect increasing accountability from grantee or contract organizations, the administrative burdens add up for nonprofit organizations. This is becoming a very big risk across the nonprofit world. What was acceptable or even a best practice a year ago may no longer apply. It's important to read the fine print in every contract or grant agreement and to keep abreast of all changes in government regulations. (This is one of the examples of risks that affect multiple areas: in this case, finance and compliance. Such risks are heightened because instead of two areas attempting to deal with the risk, each may assume the other is doing so and no one is ready to act.) Accepting contracts or grants that come with reporting or administrative requirements your organization cannot manage is a major risk for nonprofits today. Additionally, some grants and contracts require an organization to do upfront spending with reimbursement to follow. It is not unusual to hear of long reimbursement delays, mid-year changes in allowable expenses or mid-year funding reductions.

What to Watch For

From the beginning of any grant-funded project (even before the application is prepared), review and highlight grant requirements that go beyond what your organization can handle operationally. Keep in mind that grants and contracts often come with unfunded mandates—compliance, accountability or operating requirements that add administrative burden and financial risk with no funding to support them. This can become a serious issue in short order if it is not recognized early on. In particular, look for items such as:

- Accounting requirements that differ in details and timing from your existing process or procedures.
- Requirements for bonds, contingencies, insurance, legal settlements, disallowances, and other expenses, even if they will eventually be reimbursed, refunded, or waived.
- Conditions or requirements for hiring, use of consultants, multi-year leases, or operational requirements that will add to your organization's expenses.

Prevention

Preventing risks with grants, activities, and overhead includes simply deciding whether an otherwise worthwhile grant or mission-related activity is worth pursuing, or whether your organization can afford to subsidize these costs with private funds or fundraising activities. This can be an incredibly difficult choice to make, particularly if it involves withdrawing from or canceling a long-standing project or program loved by staff, the public, or clients. Assessing financial sustainability is a critical ERM activity, especially if your organization will be asked to commit to a multi-year contract or grant agreement that does not include funding for the increased cost of doing business over the term of the grant or contract.

- Does the organization have reserves, a line of credit available to smooth cash flow while waiting for reimbursement?
- Have management and board updated policies for handling reserves and borrowing on the line of credit? Does leadership understand the scope and limits of these policies? (Many organizations borrow money from contingency reserves or lines

of credit for immediate needs that will definitely be reimbursed, but if the reimbursement doesn't come, the reserve will be diminished and you may hit the cap on your line of credit and be unable to pay it down in a timely fashion.)

– Accounting for all grants or special project funding must hold up to a rigorous independent audit and meet generally accepted accounting practice standards (GAAP).

– Make certain that passwords, codes and access to your accounting system are functions handled by several staff members and that knowledge of how to use the software and generate reports is the responsibility of more than one person. Multiple people in the organization should be able to generate financial reports. Note: your password security should include a formal and protected protocol for handling a situation in which one person with a password is unavailable. A protocol based on quick reaction, "Here, use mine," is always a risk. Sharing passwords is a breach of security standards. To avoid such a situation, make certain that there is redundancy built into your processes. (Many organizations have procedures whereby an authorized user can create a temporary password to permit access without sharing passwords.)

Mitigation

It is not uncommon for an organization to discover changes to requirements or procedures by a funder when it is already working on a grant-funded project. Although both the funded organization and the funder addressed this possibility at the outset mid-year or mid-project changes —particularly when they involve changes in procedures—can still sometimes crop up.

These issues don't go away by themselves, so it is important to work together to manage the change in a way that limits damage or dislocation.

Dealing with Discretionary, Ad Hoc, and Emergency Situations

Unplanned events happen. Having resources your organization can utilize in an emergency or when a unique opportunity presents itself is essential. Experts advise budgeting three-six months of cash reserves or establishing a budget for new programming. On this point, nonprofit leaders often note that that they are already functioning in a precarious financial situation and cannot afford to put extra cash away. Absent budgeted reserves or new funding that includes resources for start-up, nonprofit leaders are left with few good options. The pressure to maintain funding for current programming, handle emergencies and impulse to take on new projects can create serious organizational tensions and can lead to choices that undermine the financial stability of a nonprofit.

What to Watch For

It may not seem possible to plan for unexpected circumstances, but it can be. There are almost always warning signs. Sometimes, the warning signs are present for such a long time that they become part of the background noise. Other times, they aren't recognized at all.

When assessing your organization's risk, as described in Part I, remember to consider likelihood and impact. Periodically review your list of risks to make certain that the likelihood that the risk will occur remains as expected previously. One reason for using an automated tool such as The Nonprofit Risk App is that you can adjust the likelihood rating so your vulnerabilities are recalculated when conditions change.

Prevention

Evaluating risk in an organization requires people who know the organization, its history, and its operations to bring their experiences to bear. Formalizing risk assessment is an essential way to monitor emerging risk or vulnerabilities. Testing systems and practices and using checklists are ways to formalize tracking of recurring risks. Another source of intelligence on risk is to solicit fresh perspectives from new employees, board members, and members of the public who may view the organization with fresh eyes. The loose doorknob or exposed wires may have "always" been like that, until it comes off in someone's hand or begins to spark and you need to find a locksmith or electrician in an emergency.

Mitigation

Having resources for emergencies doesn't always mean cash. Contingency planning for a critical event in advance can encompass a variety of strategies. For example, is possible to partner with peer organizations to provide assistance in the event of a fire, flood, or structural collapse. The details of this kind of planning depends on the organizations involved and their resources, but mutual aid for basic contingency operations for emergencies, extreme weather, loss of power, or threats to public safety can help both organizations maintain operations in an extraordinary situation.

Summary

If programs and services are the most visible representation of an organization, the financial operations are the fuel that make programs run.

Chapter 9
Fundraising

The area of fundraising offers perhaps the most significant difference between nonprofits and NGOs and commercial organizations and some of the biggest risks for organizations. It's been said that seeking funds, cultivating new donors, holding benefits and events, writing grant proposals, entering competitions, securing goods to raffle off or auction, soliciting donations through direct mail, on-line and through other portals and crafting personalized thank yous, among other fundraising and development activities consumes up to 80% of a nonprofit executive's time.

Some nonprofit organizations are fortunate to have dedicated sources of private funding. They can budget and use a portion of these assets to underwrite all or some operating or program expenses with funds that come from an endowment, investment portfolio, or bequest. Other organizations generate fundraising income from fee-based events or product sales, foundation grants, individual donor appeals and major gift campaigns, capital campaigns, direct mail and online appeals, and other activities that produce general operating support or project-restricted resources for program and operating expenses. Regardless of source, today nonprofit leaders and boards view their fundraising roles as primary. Even when a nonprofit organization has a steady source of private income or a guaranteed revenue stream set up in perpetuity, circumstances arise and things change calling into question just what guarantees and perpetuity really means. As an old saying goes, "Perpetuity is just around the corner."

Note: Chapter 8 on finance addresses financial issues and risk regardless of whether revenue comes from private or public sources. You may want to read that alongside this chapter.

Adding to the complexity, nonprofit fundraising isn't just about money. Many nonprofit organizations solicit and receive in-kind donations that are not cash. These may have monetary value but they come to the organization as a non-cash item. Two of the most common of these is the volunteer service of board members and pro bono experts and the receipt of donated goods to be used by the organization or sold to raise money for operations. (Chapter 6, "Personnel and Volunteers" has more information on this topic.) In-kind donations can be of any type that the organization accepts. Some organizations have the capacity to deploy volunteers and make use of pro bono assistance. Others can accept real estate and art or clothing and furniture donations to convert to cash for operations or distribute to program participants. Bequests can contain cash, securities and non-cash items, but donations of new or used items can be common.

DOI 10.1515/9781501505942-009

Fundraising is an area that lays risk traps that trip up many nonprofits. Managing the flow of volunteers, maintaining inventory, storing and distributing goods intended for clients, handling cash donations, tracking grants requires an organization to have dedicated personnel and formalized policies and business processes for each source of private funding. Fundraising is also among the most heavily regulated of all nonprofit activities. Despite this, stories appear regularly about fraud, malfeasance or fundraising blunders that cost nonprofits their reputations, donors and community confidence.

Fundraising for nonprofits typically involves five activities each of which brings with it its own set of risks. The activities and risks are discussed in this chapter. The activities are:

- *Working with grants and foundation funders.* The processes of getting grants, working with funders, and managing grants—once you have gotten them—can be fraught with risk. Here are some of the issues to watch for.
- *Managing donors.* The donor base (that is, the individuals who donate to your organization through events, campaigns, appeals, planned giving, or major gifts and donations) is a critical resource and risk area for many nonprofit organizations.
- *Raising money with fundraising events.* Events from gala dinners to school bake sales or charity auctions carry risks especially when events include cash transactions or transfers of material goods. Corporate giving to events often comes in the form of underwriting certain expenses or purchasing tables or tickets.
- *Capital campaigns.* Raising funds for the endowment or for a building fund and the construction or renovation that follows comes with unique risks.
- *Selling products and merchandise.* An arena for some nonprofits.

Working with Grants and Funders

For board members who are not used to working with nonprofit organizations, the whole area of fundraising can be fraught with confusion. Distinctions between general operating and restricted support are not easily understood. It can be hard to grasp the decision to request funding for general operations rather than for a specific program or activity. General support is just that—fungible resources that can be used for any budgeted expense from plumbing to printing to staff salaries. Restricted support can only be used for a dedicated purpose and is restricted in its use. General support is more flexible and easier to manage, but often donors prefer their support (and name) be associated with a specified or targeted use. Government grants are typically restricted in their use. The bookkeeping and accounting rules for the treatment of fundraising revenue are complex and often vexing to nonprofit boards and executives.

In addition to the due diligence you exercise in all areas of fundraising management, you will need to make certain that your board and staff, your volunteers, and the public from whom you solicit gifts, understand the laws, regulations and best practice in your region and your own policies and practices for fundraising. Failure to do so can jeopardize your entire operation. It is especially important to have a clear policy about how your organization raises money, how you calculate the tax deductible value of a donation and the purposes to which the donation is put.

This is particularly true if you are not experienced in the nonprofit world, and so there may be a period of adjustment. The vocabulary can be new and idiosyncratic. Here are some terms and concepts that are frequently used (and that we use throughout this book).

- *Donations.* Most nonprofit organizations solicit and receive donations to help support their operations. These donations may be treated advantageously for donors' tax purposes. Nonprofits need systems in place to manage cash, in-kind and other donations.
- *Bequests and Planned Giving.* This term is used to describe donations that are planned for the future by the donor. A common type of planned giving is a bequest codified in a will. Most planned giving is set to occur at a future date, when the donor is deceased. Commonly, the terms of a bequest are not known by the nonprofit organization ahead of time. Favorable tax treatment of donor assets is a primary driver of planned giving.
- *Foundation Grants.* Proposals may be solicited and grant funding provided under the terms of a legal agreement or contract. Grant funds are often provided under terms that specify allowable expenses with an approved budget and reporting at regular intervals. Grants can be *unrestricted*, meaning that the nonprofit organization can use them as it sees fit to further its legal purposes. Grants may be *restricted* to specific purposes, such as rebuilding a church steeple, paying for a staff position or other program expenses. In some cases, certain expenses may be specifically excluded from the grant funding. Some grants are *reimbursement* grants where the nonprofit organization does the work under the terms of the grant, and the nonprofit is then reimbursed for allowable costs. A grant of this nature typically involves timelines for deliverables and payments. These may also be referred to by other names such as pay-for-performance or fee-for-service. In all cases, these grants involve the nonprofit organization doing something for which they have to pay (salaries, contractors, materials, and so forth). Their expenses are then reimbursed by the grant.

  Grants can be simple one-time transactions for a single time-limited project, but they can also span multiple years and a broad geography and involve an ongoing relationship with the funder. Because foundation grants involve terms and conditions that are specific to the project to be funded, there is frequently discussion and negotiation between the funder and the nonprofit organization. Securing foundation grants and managing grants require formal policies, a grants management tracking system and training for staff involved.

The process of requesting funding for grants and other projects is governed by laws and regulations (for government grants) or by guidelines (foundation or corporate grants) so it's an organizational imperative to know what they are. If you are soliciting support through a competitive selection process like responding to a Request for Proposal (RFP) making a mistake or skipping a step will disqualify you from the process.

- *Fees and other payments.* Nonprofit organizations may charge for services that they provide. They may be simple and direct charges—for example, the cost of a ticket to the opera or a weekly payment for child care. Remember that space and facilities rentals can be a source of revenue, so if your organization rents out space, a weekly desk to a companion organization for its own purposes, or some other rental or service, these are revenues, and are not considered as fundraising.

In addition to these terms, there is a variety of terms for the grants and other funding opportunities. Funding opportunities (the most general term) can be in the form of requests for proposals (you respond with a proposal), grants (you respond with a grant application), and other terms. In all cases, respond as directed in the initial notification. Perhaps the most serious risk to avoid is to not reading and understanding the rules of the application including all responsibilities you will assume for the project and the deadlines for applications and the project itself. Among the common problems are neglecting to obtain a formal resolution certifying the application from your board if it is required as part of the application.

What to Watch For

Fundraising risk is typically associated with the way in which a nonprofit organization handles its accounting, valuation of donated goods, grants management and its tax treatment of events and other activities.

- Because many nonprofits need support for programs or activities that do not match foundation priorities and because the process of applying for and managing grants requires staff that an organization does not have, some nonprofits forego grant funding altogether. This can be a sensible decision, but it is one that should be revisited periodically over time because foundation grants can be an important source of funding for start-up and program innovation.
- There are cycles and timetables for most fundraising opportunities. It is common for nonprofit organizations to solicit donations from individuals at certain times of the year—at tax time, to take advantage of tax deductions for dona-

tions, or in conjunction with religious or social holidays. Many nonprofit organizations hold events at the same time each year. Foundation grantmaking also occurs on an annual calendar cycle that is usually available on its website. In the US, regional associations of grantmakers or the Foundation Center are a good source of information.

Prevention

Fundraising activities are heavily regulated and the rules vary across jurisdictions. Your fundraising policies can cover how you handle transactions, acknowledgments for gifts or special occasions, tax letters, processes for handling donated goods, grant management, solicitation calendar and event management as well as your accounting policies. Policies should align with IRS regulations, charity bureau standards and the like and be reviewed and updated regularly. Fundraising activity and financial reports should be shared with the board or board committee quarterly.

Your fundraising practices and how you work with current and potential donors can be formalized and shared with staff and new board members. In a more general sense, review all of your practices and policies and make them available to staff and board. New hires and new board members particularly need this information as quickly as possible. Many organizations have a fundraising policy manual and annual fundraising plan. Others use a quick-start document to help new members get up to speed.

Like client or recipient information, donor information that includes giving history, credit card or other method of payment detail, home address is highly confidential and requires a data security protocol to keep it safe. Similarly, it is considered best practice to inform all donors that their name, contact or other personal information will never be shared with another organization. Most annual reports include highlights of the year's activities. They can also include a list of donor names and corporate and foundation gifts.

- Does your organization have a current set of fundraising policies and procedures that align with local law or regulations?
- Do not assume that grant and donation opportunities adhere to past calendars and dates. Double-check submission deadlines for upcoming funding opportunities. This is as important for new opportunities as it is for grant renewals.
- An annual updated fundraising calendar with alerts that is shared with staff can prevent missed deadlines.
- In the case of complex grants that extend over time (and, possibly, over geographical boundaries), do you routinely review those conditions in grants for which you may be applying? Make certain that the facilities or other conditions that you need to carry out the terms of the grant are and will be available over the

course of the grant. Not managing grants properly can result in refusal of reimbursement or other penalties.

– Make sure that the terms and conditions of a grant, donation or bequest are reviewed and approved before accepting it. This includes allowable use of funds, reporting, use of donor or funder name in materials and other terms and conditions.

Mitigation

– When a problem arises with a grant's management, make certain that it is identified and dealt with as soon as you are made aware of it. These things do not go away by themselves. They happen, they should be watched for and prevented where possible.

– No matter how well-managed a grant is, its goals may not be achieved. Active management of funder relationships is key to securing private funds and maintaining them. Should you run into a problem with spending, deliverables or deadlines, notify the funder right away. If you need more time you can ask about no cost extensions or other changes to the grant. "Running out the clock" by spending the grant down when you know that you cannot meet its requirements won't make funders very happy. Surprising your funder is a risk you don't want to take.

Managing the Donor Base

Many nonprofit organizations have a core group of donors on whom they rely over time. In some cases, the donor base is considered a constant, and the amount that it raises can be the same each year. Changes happen over time, and it's important to be ready for such changes.

For example, many traditional arts and cultural organizations notice a "graying" of their traditional donors, while environmental, "green" organizations have seen an increase in their donors as a result of demographic changes.

Assuming that an organization's donor base Is constant and will always be there is a risk to be prevented. For both individual and philanthropic donors, requests for support only seem to increase, so there is always an element of competition for donations.

What to Watch For

- Do you track your donor base over time, checking for active, lapsed or deceased donors, amount of funds raised and change from year to year, and your donor demographic information? This data can help you estimate and set fundraising targets and where you might be in terms of donors and funds in the future.
- Changes to programming and services can affect your donor base because the two are tightly linked in many cases. Are you able to compare programming and service changes with changes in donor participation?
- Is the donor base diverse and large enough to be dependable? Having a single donor can be extraordinarily risky. In fact, a reliable donor base includes a mix of individual donors. Relying on donors from one industry, like financial services or manufacturing, may be risky if that sector experiences a downturn.
- Track what marketers sometimes call a *churn factor*—the amount and frequency with which people make donations or stop making donations or otherwise change their status. This concept of churning applies to staff, clients, and donors.

Prevention

- Do you know who your donors are? This means not just their names and addresses but what their interest is in your organization.
- Do you know who you would like them to be in the future (both long- and short-term)? Not only do you need to know and consider *who* they are (names and addresses) but also *what* they are (alumni, members, patients, and other demographics).
- Do you have specific fundraising plans, objectives, and goals that you track? This is particularly important for targeted fundraising such as for annual operating costs or development of a specific project.
- When donations of goods and services are offered, do you have policies in place to guide their use and acceptance? Many public libraries have a gift acceptance form that stresses that donated books are welcome (if they are) and will be used in the library's best judgment. Grandma's ragged copy of *David Copperfield* that is missing the last chapter may be donated, but the library must reserve the right to put it in a book sale or even in a dumpster. Donations of used technology equipment can be generous, but a computer that originally cost over $5,000 may have little or no value today, causing the recipient organization to basically be used as a way to dispose of the item.
- For in-kind donations, do you make it clear at the outset who determines what the value of the donated item is? In many places, the value of the donated items must be determined by the donor (not the recipient) for the purposes of the donor's tax deduction.

For technology donations, your acceptance form should clearly state that any data on the donated device has been sanitized by the donor. Most organizations provide that type of notice and resist the temptation to take responsibility for purging data from the donated device. Security experts suggest that is the donor's responsibility.

Fundraising Events

One of the areas in which nonprofits and nongovernmental organizations differ greatly in their operations and procedures is in their approaches to fundraising events.

A frequent fundraising topic of discussion is about the purpose of the event. While some people may consider an annual fundraising event to be a way of raising money, other people may consider it to be a way of bringing together supporters, board members, staff, and perhaps clients so that they can mingle with one another and informally discuss the organization and their support of it.

On the fundraising side of the discussion, some organizations hold a gala non-dinner or event to raise money. This gala non-dinner takes place at the time and place of a contributor's choosing. The "admission fee" for such a dinner is a check payable to the organization; there are no speeches and no dressing up. At the other extreme are fundraising events that become a part of a community and perhaps overshadow the organization itself. People sometimes purchase tickets to the event without an interest in the benefiting organization.

What to Watch For

- In a case where the organization or a fundraising event has a long history or role within the community, recognize that although your balance sheet may tell you that it's all about the money you raise, the fundraising event may have become a community event that is bigger than your organization. Here are some other risks you may encounter:
- It can be a challenge to match a fundraising event to the organization's mission and ethos. Sometimes the choice is to leave all the work behind and celebrate, enjoy, or otherwise be distracted (while raising money). Other times, the choice is to highlight the organization with, perhaps, a special speaker or presentation.
- In the case of repeating events (perhaps annual fundraisers), approach changes cautiously, particularly if the annual event is the one time when many people interact with the organization. Considering cost versus funds raised may help with the decisions.

– Make certain that the invitations and tickets to fundraising events separate out and detail the cost of the direct benefit to the donor from the amount of the ticket. This is required for reporting and tax purposes and can also help donors consider their priorities.

Mitigation

With a large group of people, some will not be able to attend the event. Consider reaching out to people who you know will be unable to attend to fill them in on what will happen (or has happened) at the event so that they appreciate that they are part of the group. Otherwise, you run the risk of making them feel unwelcome. That is merely bad manners, but if people who feel unwelcome start to express that thought with their donations (or by sharing their opinion with others) you have created an unnecessary risk.

Summary

Nonprofit organizations are responsible for making certain that adequate resources are available for them to carry out their mission. Overall responsibility usually resides with the board and chief executive with assistance from staff and/or volunteers in a Development Department.

As you have seen in this chapter, revenue can be generated from planned events or from donations and grants. Each of these sources has its own risks; they share the common aspect that, in most ways, they are only issues for nonprofits and non-governmental organizations.

Chapter 10
Marketing, Communications, and Reputation

Through your marketing, communications, and reputation, you present your organization to the world. Your organization's identity, brand, and reputation go beyond your mission. They showcase your value to the community and distinguish your organization from all others. The environment in which nonprofits and NGOs operate is on a 24/7, 365-day cycle. Staff, board members, and service users can opine on their experience with your organization in real time, and news of bad practices, critical incidents, and poor working conditions can instantly go viral.

Making the case for strongly managed messaging and reputation management goes beyond a risk framework. It is an essential organizational function for driving strategy, increasing reach, and ensuring high performance. Failure to actively monitor your marketing, internal and external communications, or reputation can create vulnerabilities that can quickly become liabilities when something goes awry. And something always goes wrong.

As described in Part I of the book, every functional area of a nonprofit organization carries risks that may seem trivial on their own. It's only when you dig deeper to assess the likelihood and impact of a specific risk or consider risk interactions that the actual degree of risk fully emerges. Remember that, at any given point in time, an unattended risk interacting with changing circumstances can combine in ways that are highly damaging.

To avoid being surprised by risks that are unfamiliar today and catastrophically real tomorrow, you have to have a basic understanding of each risk. You must continually monitor each risk's likelihood and impact as the conditions of your organization change. Not only should you monitor these risks regularly over time to manage them as your organization changes, but you should also adopt a method of risk assessment that allows you to model various scenarios and correct stressors that can create conditions in which your organization can succeed or fail.

Tip: A tool such as The Nonprofit Risk App can help in weighing risks present in each functional area of operation and in letting you do testing (what-if gaming) in different scenarios.

DOI 10.1515/9781501505942-010

The five major areas of risk described in this chapter are commonly associated with communication. These areas are:

- *Focusing on mission and partners.* What you say and do, as well as whom you do it with and for, are the basics of your communications and fundraising activities. You may take those communications as given (or just assume that someone else in the organization has dealt with them). Both fundraising and communication personnel need to be clear on these issues because, if something goes wrong, they are likely to be the first point of angry contact, along with the staff, board, and media.
- *Calendaring.* Managing the organization's calendar and events to avoid conflicts, as well as managing interactions and synergies across all events and parts of the organization.
- *Messaging.* Creating and disseminating organization-wide messages that are relevant, consistent, factual, and powerful.
- *Managing the economic model.* Communication activities can be used to support the organization as a whole, but they can also be used to generate income for the organization.
- *Outsourcing.* Communication is frequently outsourced in whole or in part to contractors, other organizations, and volunteers.

Focusing on Mission and Partners

It's hard to conceive of a nonprofit organization that does not have a clearly established mission, but such is the case more often than you would like to think. Commercial corporations are generally regarded as having the purpose of maximizing shareholder value. Although there are many discussions about the details and nuances of this purpose, however you view it, the purpose of a commercial corporation stands in contrast to that of a nonprofit organization or government. In these organizations, some public purpose is often the mission or goal.

What to Watch For

Here is a list of things to consider as you look for risks in your mission and in your work with partnering organizations. It's not exhaustive, and your organization may need to occasionally modify it. It can be a useful starting point for you in creating your own watch list.

- Monitor mission and purposes as times change. It's not enough to have a nice mission statement on the wall. Over the years as conditions of specific funding gifts and donations change and as the organization's environment and needs change, the mission and purpose may change. In addition, as in commercial organizations, laws and regulations may impact the operations and even the mission of a nonprofit.

– Keep track of grant conditions. With fundraising, it is critical to balance the conditions attached to gifts and bequests, including those that may not materialize for years or even decades. These conditions can apply to operations and communications. Particularly as time goes on, an organization can easily accumulate a wide array of conditions that can affect almost every part of the organization.

– Track related organizations and their risks. In addition to missions and conditions, nonprofit organizations run risks when they form formal or informal relationships with other nonprofit or commercial organizations. These relationships can come with conditions either at the beginning or they can develop over time. Furthermore, if related organizations run into any problems—from operational and financial issues to reputational concerns—their problems can affect your organization.

– In addition to risk, track changes in names and missions of your partners who either provide you with services or who are funders. If a partner's mission is refined in a way to exclude your funding, don't be surprised.

– Remember that a "change" in a partner's priorities and mission may be a new director or board's interpretation of long-standing priorities and the mission.

– Do you keep a constantly updated list of the correct names, addresses, spellings, and positions or titles for your own organization and partnering organizations? If you use an integrated contact management database, make certain that it can handle the same person being listed in multiple roles at multiple organizations. Ideally, it should also have a date range to apply for each item of contact management.

– Do you periodically review board minutes from partnering organizations or have a person attend as a liaison? This is an area of particular vulnerability when the organizations are different sizes.

Prevention

The first step in preventing risks related to mission and partners is to know the terms of your mission and conditions, and to be diligent in working with partner organizations and donors. One particular area of risk is from longstanding projects and relationships that have not been looked at carefully for years. New management in the nonprofit organization may appropriately question conditions that have been handed down that may either no longer apply or may have evolved in the passing down.

Management in donor and partner organizations may also change. If so, it may be appropriate to reevaluate the conditions and purposes relevant to their funding.

These evaluations can be positive and productive, but it is not uncommon for them to be unpleasant. You may deal with donors as organizations or donors as individuals (including heirs of deceased donors). As in so many risk areas, the most effective way of preventing risk events is to know the details. Particularly with projects and relationships that date back a long time, there may be a reluctance to do this, but it is essential.

Staying abreast of conditions in your partnering organizations is not enough; you need to stay abreast of conditions in their partners' organizations. Beyond that, staying on top of issues that are bubbling up in any of the spheres that you or your partners work in may help prepare you for problems as well as knowing the concerns to check for.

One of the most difficult steps to take in preventing risk events from mission and partners is to prevent future problems. This means clarifying terms and conditions of any grants or gifts and reviewing them for their impact on operations now and in the future. (Many nonprofit organizations are able to work with donors and potential donors to minimize restrictions, but it may be too late for some agreements from the past.)

Mitigation

When a risk related to mission and conditions or partners arises, the first step (as always) is to find out the details. This is a very good argument for conducting periodic audits of missions of partners so that you are finding problems before they become crises.

When the risk event occurs in a partner (or even is alleged to occur in a partner), your ability to find out what is going on may be limited. Your own communication tools should be ready to respond to your own and related organizations' problems with a response protocol that is independent of the specific partner and issue.

Calendaring

The public-facing components of your organization, both fundraising and communication, are involved with *calendaring*, the scheduling and management of events for the public. Internal events or events that involve external players rather than the general public can pose the biggest challenges.

Non-public events with external players

We make a distinction between public events that are open to a broad group of people and events that need to be scheduled with external players such as clients, funders, suppliers, and users of the organization. Typically, events with external players (but not the general public) are conducted as part of the ongoing operations of the organization.

Among the biggest challenges in event planning and scheduling are those that involve conflicts with other events. The broader your potential audience for an event, the more likely you are to have a conflict. Risk comes into the picture when conflicts aren't taken into account in a timely manner.

All organizations have calendaring issues and potential conflicts both internally and externally.

What to Watch For

Knowing that all organizations have some kind of calendaring issue can actually make your risk analysis easier. It's there: you just have to find it. And once you find the first one, chances are you'll find others that exist or might exist if you don't take action.

– A companion to events that "everyone knows about" is events that no one knows about. Usually this is accidental because they may be scheduled at the rushed ending of a meeting after everyone has either physically or mentally left the meeting.

– Events where the location or time excludes critical individuals or classes of individuals, unless that is a deliberate strategic goal as in the case of reshaping a board's membership to exclude certain individuals or groups of individuals. (You might call this "strategic calendaring" because the scheduling prevents certain individuals or groups from attending or voting.)

– Make certain that project- and grant-specific calendar events and associated notifications are held so that grant funding is not jeopardized. This is a particular issue for many nonprofit organizations because funding can be tied to the calendar events, even though the events themselves do not generate funding.

– Repeating scheduled events that "everyone knows about" so they aren't listed on any calendars.

Prevention

Centralizing calendaring and scheduling in an organization may appear to be the simplest way to avoid conflicts, but it is remarkable how difficult that can be. Some degree of decentralized scheduling is essential. Making an appointment for a plumber to deal with a clogged drain is irrelevant to many parts of an organization, but it's critical to the people in the vicinity of the drain, and the plumber may rightly take priority over any and all other events.

Cloud-based scheduling products such as calendar software from Alphabet (Google), Apple, Microsoft, CiviCRM, and Salesforce are not a cure-all; for individuals, their calendars need to be integrated with personal appointments and other commitments. It helps (as do collaborative scheduling tools such as Doodle), but these calendaring products are not a total solution.

What is possible is to delineate what types of scheduling are handled in what parts of the organization. It is not necessary to expose the reasons for blocked-out time, but sharing unavailable times and getting people to use those tools is helpful.

Be particularly sensitive to scheduling volunteers and external players. One of the reasons volunteers leave nonprofit projects is that the demands on their time become excessive.

For regions where weather can be a problem, scheduling an alternate date along with the primary date can save a lot of time. In regions with harsh winter weather, such alternate dates are often automatically scheduled for all events between December and March.

Provide multiple contact routes for people to change their attendance status or ask questions. This is particularly important when events are scheduled during in-person meetings.

Mitigation

As soon as a conflict is evident, handle it—it won't go away by itself. The organization needs to speak with one voice and, with regard to calendaring, that voice needs to be reliable.

Know who can reschedule an event, so that if a conflict becomes apparent (whether it's weather, or availability of a critical participant or a conference area), the meeting can either be rescheduled or planned without the conflicted participant.

Messaging

The organization needs to have clearly set message protocols so that people inside and outside the organization know who is speaking and with what voice (personal voice, corporate voice, internal communication, and so forth).

What to Watch For

As is often the case with risks, there are some early warning signs you can watch for.
- Letterhead, website, and social media messages that by their nature (design, originating account, and so forth) carry the weight of the organization. To use Twitter terminology, the difference between a message marked with #ourOrganization, and another sent from @ourOrganization indicates that the first is *about* the organization, but the second is *from* the organization.
- Because letterhead, social media accounts, and websites are the hallmarks of official messaging, make certain that they are controlled as carefully as cash, keys, and other valuables.
- Be particularly careful with new media accounts that often are first developed on an ad hoc basis and become an official channel of communication without protocols being built around them.
- Ask for copies of the final result of media releases and articles. This is particularly important for media that you may not deal with regularly. In the case of photos and videos that are part of interviews, assume from the start that you will want to reuse them.
- Not everyone who works on communication has the same knowledge and background. Take nothing for granted and make sure that everyone who deals with media knows to ask these questions:
    o Are you on a deadline?
    o How much information do you want? (Words, minutes, etc.)
    o Is there a photo component? In this day of powerful cell phones, a simple interview can easily be a photo shoot, so make certain that people are ready.

Prevention

In today's world, it's critical to be able to identify who speaks for an organization in what contexts, as well as in what role and, most importantly, for what organization.

Note: This is an area that is rapidly changing as this is written as new media and social platforms are arising.

Once you have identified the speaker, the role, and the organization, in today's world it's necessary to know the rules by which all participants are playing. Do they recognize the roles as you do so that they know who is speaking in what capacity?

For many organizations, it is not unreasonable to have a simple chart that documents who officially speaks for which topics. Post it on your website for media and the public to refer to. Creating such a contact chart is an excellent exercise for an organization (large or small) because it brings the issues to the forefront where you may be able to get consensus.

Also in the area of prevention, establish a protocol for managing the information about the people and organizations with which you operate. The protocol can include who is responsible, as well as rules for managing changes and updates to data. If a major funder of your organization has a new address or other new descriptive or contact information, does someone handle it informally or are there rules for determining who makes the changes and when they are made?

Mitigation

When messaging has gone wrong—whether it's messaging from the outside about your organization, anonymous messaging that mentions your organization in passing, or messaging that for one reason or another is sent from your organization incorrectly or, perhaps with errors—you need to be able to quickly identify exactly what has happened.

For larger organizations that, unfortunately, need to deal with these incidents on a frequent basis, a formal checklist used for identifying the problem can be coupled with specific protocols for handling each combination of factors. For even the smallest organization, a similar but smaller checklist can help people find their way in the world of message management. Preparing such a checklist and associated response protocols can be a powerful advance mitigation strategy for even the smallest organization.

Tip: Don't just use the checklist to identify messaging issues. Save the incident checklists so that you can track messaging risk events. Particularly for smaller organizations, it is easy to take each event as a one-time rarity. Keeping the data can help you identify patterns. Also make certain to include a follow-up note with each checklist so that you can keep track of actions taken and, very importantly, information that may come to light after the incident has passed. In this regard, it is useful to record and keep contemporaneous records of what happened, whether or not those records are modified by subsequent events or analysis.

For organizations large or small, you can construct a checklist from any of these factors that are appropriate. You may want to use this checklist for messages sent to and from your organization whenever there is some question about the nature of the message (that is, whether it is accurate or not).

– Message source name: identified and known: Y/N?
– Message source location: internal/external/unknown?
– Message response protocol used (social media, web, letterhead, responsibility for response, etc.)?
– Does the message indicate a breach of security?
– Is the content damaging? (This answer needs to be tracked over time as the risk event plays out.)
– Is a response required?
– Who will respond?
– If the decision is not to reply, who will provide and enforce that silence?
– Does the message contain threats?
– What other parties are brought in?
– Remember to track consequences and subsequent events.

Managing the Economic Model

An organization's activities have value to the organization itself, society, employees, recipients, and others. In commercial organizations, the value of endeavors can easily be measured by the profit and loss data for each activity.

In both commercial and other organizations, some projects and expenses are integrated into the overall budget without showing separate profit and loss data. In all organizations, management is looking at whether specific activities should be self-supporting.

This particularly arises with regard to activities in communications. Is a website that contains valuable information a resource that should be available for a fee? For some nonprofits, the publication of books and periodicals has generated positive cash flow. In discussing communications these days, the question of what can or should be a priced service is critical.

This is a question that is both financial and essential to the organization's role. The discussion is listed here because there is risk involved in almost every decision that is made with regard to charging (or not charging) for information that an organization publishes, whether it is created by the organization or assembled from research.

Perhaps the biggest risk in deciding on an economic model for an organization's intellectual property (and "free" is an economic model) is that publication in the age of the Internet is dramatically and rapidly changing. That, in and of itself, is a major risk.

What to Watch For

- Do the organization's publication and data creation activities constitute an essential activity or service? Is it a traditional and long-standing activity that is not essential, or has the entire publication and data creation process become irrelevant in the web-based world? (All of the above are possible answers to these questions, but, if these are your answers, make certain that you actually do follow through on each component.)
- Because the web is truly worldwide, does this mean that the organization's audience (and potential customers) for its intellectual property is global? Does this affect the creation and publication processes? Do translation issues need to be addressed?
- Is it necessary to create a planned scenario of change and evolution reflecting consumers of the intellectual property and their relationship to technology? (Age, for example, is a major factor.)
- "Publication" isn't just about brochures, websites, and white papers. It can cover the development, use, and protection of the organization's intellectual property (see "Prevention" in the following section for more details).
- Another area of risk is the fact that information that an organization may previously have charged for (often in print) is now often available for free. More than one organization (commercial, governmental, or nonprofit) has seen its revenue stream disappear with the advent of open data.

Prevention

Just about every organization has intellectual property among its assets. How you create, manage, and protect that intellectual property is up to you and your board.

The key parts of your organization's brand and presence—such as logos and slogans—are valuable to you and others. Consult a legal advisor for advice on how to protect these properties in your jurisdiction. International treaties governing trademarks and copyrights can be expensive to work with, but an experienced legal advisor willing to sit for half an hour with your executive director and/or board can provide advice that is customized and scaled to your organization. There are some basic steps that you can take that are not expensive in many cases.

Caution: These laws, regulations, and treaties vary by location, so make certain you seek advice from someone who knows where you are located and is familiar with your situation. Beware of searching the web for advice on this subject, because it may be outdated or applicable to another area. In the global Internet world, you need to consider the location of your readers and audience as well as your own.

Your staff and board should have a general understanding of the issues involving intellectual property so that your organization does not infringe upon the rights of other people and organizations. Ongoing training should remind people of their responsibilities under the law.

Mitigation

There are two types of risk events that arise regarding your intellectual property.
- *Unauthorized use by others.* If your intellectual property (logo, published materials, and the like) is used without your permission, it is usually a good idea to notify the unauthorized user and take appropriate action. Many organizations have a standard procedure and form letter (usually written by a legal advisor) that are used as a first-stage response. Informal use of your intellectual property needs to be thought through before an incident occurs.
- *Your use of others' property.* If you have mitigated the issue with training, as advised in the previous section, this shouldn't occur. Nevertheless, it can happen. If you discover that your organization has accidentally infringed on intellectual property owned by someone else, an immediate response (such as stopping that use) is appropriate. Depending on the scope of the misuse, you may need to bring in legal counsel very early on in the process so that you (and your staff, funders, clients, and patrons) are not surprised.

When it comes to your economic model itself, this needs to be monitored and addressed in the same way as in a commercial organization. Keeping track of the environment for the business or service is just as essential for a nonprofit as for a commercial organization because the basic issues are the same. There are many resources—including publications, websites, conferences, and consultants—you can use. It is often a good idea to explicitly search for commercial operation strategies related to your economic model so that you get a broader perspective on the issues.

Summary

Marketing, communications, and reputation are among the fastest changing aspects of the modern Internet-based world. Many people and organizations still rely on comfortable ideas along the lines of "our users/supporters/clients won't be interested in those technologies."

Many mission statements guide the nonprofit organization to instruct, support, or communicate in advancement of a cause or activities. The tools that are needed today are different from those of yesterday, but the mission of communication remains valid and must be implemented in new ways.

Chapter 11
Operations

The area of organizational operations may be the single functional area that most closely resembles its counterpart in commercial and governmental organizations. If programs and services are the most visible parts of a nonprofit organization, operations (sometimes referred to as *back-office operations*) are the functions that make programs and services work. Keeping the lights on and the plumbing working are just as important for nonprofit organizations as for any other organization, but, despite the similarities, there are some differences. This chapter identifies some of those differences; it also highlights the main operational areas of risk that you should be focusing on.

Handling Operational Tax Issues in Nonprofit and Nongovernmental Organizations

Depending on the structure of the organization, its location, and the governing laws and regulations, it may be eligible to receive public funding either directly or in the form of tax benefits. These laws and regulations can be complex—organizations large and small often have difficulty sorting through them. A further complication is that accountants and managers may be experienced in commercial enterprises, but in working with nonprofits, they may need to review specific issues. (And, just to make things more complicated, the laws and regulations themselves tend to change.)

Note: Chapter 13, "Board Governance and Oversight," has a high-level overview of organizational structures.

What to Watch For

Basic eligibility for certain benefits, tax abatements and exemptions, and other advantages of nonprofit organizations can require significant amounts of time. Although each benefit is different, there is a basic set of steps to take:
1. *Investigate* what is available.
2. *Provide documentation* as required to register for the benefit.
3. *Handle routine updates* as necessary (perhaps on an annual basis or, in the case of sales and use taxes, on a case-by-case basis).

DOI 10.1515/9781501505942-011

Sometimes these benefits are sizable and significant; in other cases, the benefits are small. They can be so small that it is easy to dismiss them, but this decision should not be taken lightly.

As an example, consider a situation in which a nonprofit organization is exempt from sales or use taxes for its purchases within a state or other area. If the tax rate is 10%, and the cost of a package of 500 sheets of blank paper is $4.50, the amount of tax works out to 45¢. To take advantage of that exemption (in the amount of 45¢), the organization must provide documentation of its tax-exempt status. While some organizations and staff may find it tedious to carry the tax exemption certification or to keep track of receipts, many organizations that that buy in bulk or purchase goods and equipment regularly can save thousands of dollars each year.

Prevention

On the other hand, if you consider the benefit over time once the initial work is done, it can mount up. Because the amounts can be small, there is often a temptation to forego the paperwork. This can be compounded when volunteers or staff who don't see the long-term consequences handle small purchases—they may even offer to pay the tax themselves. The organization, its staff, and its volunteers need discipline in tracking down and using small benefits such as these.

Tip: Sometimes the initial paperwork to set up a nonprofit account with a vendor can be daunting both for the vendor and the organization. However, there are anecdotal reports from many organizations, staff, and volunteers that local vendors may be more helpful in setting up such accounts in the hope of attracting additional local business. At the other end, some large companies also have preferred customer practices that help set up such accounts.

Mitigation

In general, once transactions have occurred, it can be difficult to recover credits or benefits that were not applied. Prevention, as noted in the previous section, is the best approach. Also, if there is a mistake made and it is caught quickly (the same day, in many cases), the initial transaction can be undone and replaced by a more beneficial one.

Reviewing Basic Operational Risks for Organizations: Document and Data Retention

Document and data retention is a challenge for most organizations. Now that so much information is digitized, the problem may even be greater than it was before. Digitized documents take up almost no space, but you may wind up maintaining documents and data that are excessive in terms of what is useful or necessary.

What to Watch For

Here are some of the basic risks that you should watch for and try to prevent. The first may seem counterintuitive, but experience has shown that it is accurate that the organization is saving excessive documents and data. This is not just a matter of space but a matter of the time spent in cataloging and searching for documents that may or may not exist.

Watch for efforts involving lots of time and frustration in trying to find a specific document or piece of information. Whether it is a manual system search for a physical document with the claim, "I know it's here somewhere," or an automated document or text search, it is often the unsuccessful search that proves that you are saving too much.

In fact, in many cases, saving too much is not the problem—the problem is that you do not have a usable document and data retention and retrieval system.

Prevention

When setting up information retention policies (paper-based or digital), start from the end of the process: don't save anything you don't need. If you don't know why you are saving a document or data (and there is no external requirement that you save it), chances are that it doesn't need to be saved. Address this both as a policy issue and as practice: do what you say you will do in terms of document retention. (Somehow, "just in case" often seems to triumph over a retention policy involving when to not keep documents.) In setting up your information retention (and elimination) policies, consult all interested parties including legal counsel, and review outstanding agreements, contracts, and regulations so that you are in compliance with all of them. Fortunately, setting this policy need not be done on a regular basis. Once it's done, you just make sure that the practice is carried out.

Note: "It may come in handy one day" is not a good reason to save documents or data.

When documents and data are saved, each item should have some type of categorization attached to it.

- What is the document or data?
- Who can see it?
- How long does that access permission last?
- Who can revise it?
- How long does that revision permission last?
- Who can discard it?
- How long does that discard permission last?
- Where is the document or data located?
- What passwords are needed?

Whether the retained data is digital or paper-based, it usually makes sense to manage the above document information on a spreadsheet or in a database. That way, you can quickly find all documents or data with permissions that are about to expire. You can also update the contact information for people who have access.

In implementing a retention policy along these lines, you may come into contact with people who point out that too much information is provided for a simple one-page document. The counterpoint to that objection is that if it's worth preserving, this information about the single one-page document is worth entering.

Note: This argument doesn't always work, but it's worth a try. The point is to save what is necessary and nothing more as well as to know why you are saving anything that is being saved.

Reviewing Basic Operational Risks for Organizations: Disaster Recovery

Disasters happen, and there isn't much you can do about them. In retrospect, you may be able to ascribe the disasters to preventable actions, but for the most part, these disasters are unforeseen and unstoppable. The traditional disasters of flood, fire, plague, and warfare have been joined by newer disasters such as climate change and cyber warfare (hacking and cyber malware that is controlled and launched by state actors or nations).

Although you cannot prevent disasters, you can plan for them and for the recovery or mitigation steps that will be needed.

What to Watch For

The line between a catastrophe or disaster and a misfortune or accident is clear only to the parties involved. There are some words and phrases you should listen for that can help you prepare for the inevitable disasters you may face. Red flags and alarms should go off when you hear remarks such as these:
- "We're lucky it wasn't worse."
- "At least it happened on a weekend."

These and similar remarks may indicate that you don't have an adequate mitigation strategy in place. On the contrary, listen happily to remarks such as, "We just used the plan and started seeing clients and running all operations by the next day."

As with every risk event you encounter in either your own organization or other organizations, consider each risk event an opportunity for learning and testing your own preparedness.

Precautions

The kind of disasters discussed in this section go beyond a single organization. In your planning for disasters, you should be providing for off-site backups of critical data as well as off-site functionality for digital operations (often with a cloud component). You should think about how to manage if your organization is without Internet or telephone access, or if the entire building is without power.

For disaster preparedness, you should start thinking about what to do if the entire region is without power. Flood waters may subside after a period of time, but if they leave behind destroyed bridges and tunnels over a wide area, no one may be able to move without effort. To find any kind of usable facility for your operations, you may be looking at severe disruptions.

Your clients, employees, patrons, vendors, and other people you deal with may be similarly unreachable or unable to get anywhere they want to go. A disaster preparedness plan can help you to a certain extent, but a lot of your actual disaster management may have to be built as needed.

The main component must be the ability for people to work together in new and different configurations. If they can do that, the disaster's damage can be managed as best as possible.

There is another key point to a successful disaster recovery plan: It should be triggered automatically. It is human nature to think that just one more turn of the screw or one more attempt at trying to start a car engine might do the trick. Having a rigorous protocol that switches you over to alternative operations can prevent these kinds of moment-to-moment attempts to try to make things work.

Preparing for Business Interruption

These are among the most common types of business interruptions you should pre-pare for.

What to Watch For

You can group business interruption risks into groups as follows:

- *Acts and accidents.* Watch for acts of malice or fraud such as outright theft of items, deliberate diversion of funds, disruptions of operations, or similar actions.
- *Operational errors.* To the fullest extent possible, prepare for operational errors by anyone you employ or deal with. Without malicious intent, people may make mistakes or perform improperly, perhaps due to circumstances outside the work-place.
- *Problems with partners.* Do not assume that partner organizations work properly. For example, balancing the company checking account monthly is a routine and essential process. Periodically validating the statement data that you receive is prudent, particularly in investment accounts.
- *Problems with people.* Essential people, whether as part of your organization, part of partner organizations, or any group with which you deal (including financial advisors, funders, and regulators), may not be able to adequately perform their work. Are you prepared for this?
- *Location changes of partners.* Many partners (suppliers, consultants, and others) have established relationships that sometimes have been based on location. It is not uncommon in working with nonprofit organizations to discover long-stand-ing relationships originally based on location (for example, the near-by office supply store) but where both parties have moved. Although the location no longer is convenient, the value of the long-standing relationship and knowledge on both sides may be worth keeping things as is. However, it is worth reviewing location-based relationships from time to time.

Handling Failure of Key Partners

This is one of the most frightening operational problems any organization can expe-rience. If you rely on a single organization for the bulk (or all) of your funding, and they close unexpectedly, what do you do?

If your organization relies on another organization for its operational support or guidance, what do you do if the organization closes or cannot function?

What to Watch For

There are two basic approaches to prepare for this kind of problem.

The first is to limit sole sources or unique partners. This may or may not be an appropriate or feasible strategy for your organization. What is important is to recognize that it can pose a risk. Evaluate if such a risk exists, and, if it does, how it can be mitigated.

If your support is not just financial, the failure of a partnering organization can be just as traumatic as the death of a close friend or relative. Who do you turn to for guidance and support? Who knows you and your organization well enough to bring up an issue that you don't know about that might affect you down the road?

The second approach is not to have two sources for critical resources, but to have a backup resource that can step in quickly. This might be another nonprofit in the same field, but perhaps located hundreds or thousands of miles away. Such contingency backup plans can be mutually advantageous.

Summary

As you hear about problems that affect various organizations, try to learn from what you hear. The first step is to not ask, "Could that happen here?" but rather, asking, "*How* could that happen here?"

The point is that *anything* could happen *anywhere*. You do your best to forestall problems, but if you start from the premise that anything can happen under the right circumstances, the challenge becomes finding what those circumstances might be. In order to do that, you need to look carefully at your organization and how it functions. (You also have to keep finding out the details of what has happened elsewhere, because the first reports are often revised.)

Delving into the details of what happened and how it could happen in your environment doesn't allow a quick "Yes" or "No," the simple (and not particularly useful) responses to, "Could that happen here?"

Chapter 12
Technology & Data

A nonprofit organization's technology and data functions may be managed by a central department, decentralized to functional divisions of the organization, or outsourced to an outside vendor. Each approach to managing and supporting your organization's technology needs comes with its own set of risks. Largely because of cost and limits on technology funding in government contracts and foundation grants, too many nonprofit organizations depend on older hardware and multiple, dated software platforms. The drag caused by aging technology affects organization performance and the ability to generate data and reports. These elements taken together create an environment that is ripe for risk.

Nonprofits may be more prone to technology risks because of the high cost of technology and the people needed to support and manage it. Technology and the data it produces interact in ways that pose very specific risks to nonprofit organizations.

The risks for six major activities are described in this chapter:
– Staying on top of cyber continuity.
– Working with organization-wide systems and standards.
– Maintaining functional systems and standards.
– Keeping in touch with web and social media.
– Organizing hardware, networks, and devices.
– Developing and acquiring systems, data, apps, and projects.

Staying on Top of Cyber Continuity

If white papers, conferences, training seminars, and articles in the media are any indication, everyone is concerned about security in the digital world. If they are an indication, it's a misleading one. Too often, the discussion is about a rare but catastrophic event rather than drilling deeper into the more common and ordinary events that pose potentially more damaging risks every day.

Cyber continuity is the term used to encompass all of the activities and policies that center on one simple idea: you should be able to depend on your technology resources to work tomorrow just as you do today. Interruptions and disruptions in your organization's access to and use of necessary technology are a growing concern for nonprofit leaders and boards. Regardless of the source of the disruption – hackers, faulty hardware, user error, power outage, extreme weather or malfeasance – the impact of rendering an organization unable to access or use its technology is reason enough to have a cyber continuity plan and off-site or cloud based data storage.

DOI 10.1515/9781501505942-012

What matters is keeping your technology available for use and functioning well. Once you are confident about that, you can take other steps to improve it.

What to Watch For

There are three primary considerations for cyber continuity in an organization:

- *Cyber and technology asset management.* Know what your technology environment and resources are. What are they, where are they, and who owns them? (This last question is very important in the age of BYOD—bring your own device.) For each device, you should know the usual inventory details (serial number, model number, and so on). Remember that software is just as much an asset as hardware. A difference is that whereas physical devices usually have a serial number apiece, when it comes to software licenses, they often apply to a certain number of devices but not to specific devices or users. (See the section later in this chapter on cyber security for specific risks.)

  A plan is needed to manage software updates across your organization. Many software upgrades are in fact corrections of errors and patches for newly discovered bugs. Not updating hardware and software can open your data systems to viruses, bugs and hacking, perhaps the most common risk to cyber continuity.

  Staff need to be familiar with and receive training on your organization's technology plan and platforms, to ensure that people know what resources they have and how to use them. From sign in passwords and calendaring meetings to using shared drives and laptops, the amount of time organizations spend responding to technology complaints and user issues or fiddling with document formatting and frozen spreadsheets can be enormous.

- *Contingency planning.* Have procedures and a response protocol in place that are known, practiced, and taught so that regularly occurring issues can be dealt with quickly and managed in an orderly manner. Remember that the goal is continuity, which means addressing the small issues so that when an unusual event occurs, your resources can be deployed to resolve it.

- *Cyber security.* Knowing what your real cyber security risks are is essential to finding and mitigating them.

Note: The Year 2000 Problem is now widely considered to have been much ado about nothing. In fact, it is a wonderful example of the successful identification and remediation of a very serious problem. For its reputation now to be much ado about nothing is a textbook example of success in identifying, managing, and mitigating risk.

- Do you provide staff and others with regular training and refreshers on how to use your organization's equipment, data systems and software?

- Do you have a formal procedure for authorizing access to organization data and technology and means to prevent sharing passwords or log-ins?
- Moving from one way of managing technology (centralized to decentralized) or from one software platform to another, can create vulnerabilities as people adjust to the new ways of working or new responsibilities. Shifting to bring your own device (BYOD) or work-at-home arrangements, means reconfiguring devices or setting up remote access. Do you incorporate time and energy for tasks associated with changing technologies?
- Do you make certain that systems and can handle required data and formats for current and potential partners and funders whose data standards and formats must be used for submission of reports and invoices for projects and grant funding.
- Implementation of systems and policy standards requires expert technology staff or pro bono volunteers. Does your organization's budget cover the staffing costs and resources needed to support users, keep the systems running, respond to emergencies, insure the accuracy of the information and data collected and generate reports?
- Do you sanitize devices that are being discarded so that data and security credentials are not given away?

Prevention

Make certain your inventories of hardware and software functionality are up to date. These inventories should include serial numbers, current versions, and support contacts both inside the organization and at vendors. This is always difficult in a BYOD world, but being able to answer the question prompted by a news headline "Can this happen here?" can be critical.

Mitigation

The primary mitigation goal is simple: get things running again. Have procedures in place so that the analysis of what happened can proceed during and after the restoration of service. Being able to simultaneously restore service and perform necessary post-incident reviews can help move both activities forward.

Working with Organization-wide Systems and Standards

These include centralized databases, organization-wide software for activities such as budgeting, time sheets, and other operational issues. To facilitate the optimal functioning and proper use of your organization-wide systems, it is useful to have a set of operating policies and regular training and supervision of system administrators and users regarding the required protocols, formats, and devices that are used for those operations.

In short, the advantages of organization-wide systems and policy standards focus on the clarity and consistency it provides across the organization. The disadvantage is centered on the fact that standards can inhibit innovation and improvement if users become complacent about doing things in one way only.

Although there is a popular idea that technology moves rapidly and constantly, in fact, advances in technology most often occur in steps and jolts rather than continual improvement. Among the major lurches forward of the last few decades have been the rise of mobile devices, the use of the Internet (in the very late 1980s), the rise of the web (with 1995 being considered a pivotal moment for end-users to become aware of the web), new security standards for the web that enable online banking and financial transactions, and explosion of social media. It typically takes a decade or more for each of these major advances to become commonly used; to the extent that nonprofit organizations may function with very limited budgets, they may be a generation or more behind the current best practices, and that is a risk because advances since the late 1990s often have tightened up security.

Prevention

Update device and software inventories and train people in the use and maintenance of their hardware and software and platforms including BYOD (bring your own device hardware and software).

Provide a protocol for handling exceptions to the organization-wide policy standards so that they can be requested and reviewed appropriately.

Mitigation

Keep track of allowed exceptions to organization-wide standards and review them periodically to determine if the exceptions or standards need updating.

Maintaining Functional Systems and Standards

Most nonprofits use multiple data systems for different functions. For example, financial management, fundraising, client and donor relationship management, client case management and other systems needed to manage the organization's business. Many nonprofit organizations use client relationship management or case record systems. In some organizations these systems can stand alone, while in others the client experience and organization is better served when the systems work directly with one another. It is not uncommon for different departments to use specialized data plat-forms. A single client or user data system or financial management platform is often used across an organization's programs and departments. Many organizations switch back and forth between organization-wide and department systems not only over time but even in the course of routine operations. There is risk and expenses to con-sider switching environments and standards, but that has to be weighed against the benefits of using different systems that may have other benefits.

What to Watch For

In larger organizations, the existence of multiple systems can hinder the reassign-ment and transfer of staff because different areas of the organization use different systems and the skills and expertise are not shared with other members of the organization.

Prevention

Using a variety of software and data systems is commonplace in nonprofit organiza-tions today. The ideal state is when technology works to support the business needs and operations of the organization, and, more important, it provides management and staff with useful data and reports.

Here are some challenges to watch out for.
- Make certain that the goals and objectives of the organization and each unit are in sight so that discussions are about them, not about the tools being used. It's very easy to turn discussions that should be about business process or perfor-mance into discussions about the adequacy or inadequacy of technology tools
- As software systems and platforms evolve, their functionality is improved and new features and capacities are added so that a product that was perfect for one function yesterday, such as maintaining a mailing list, may become a full-fea-tured relationship management product tomorrow. Designate personnel and task them with staying current on the full functionality of the software and data platforms you use and updating user training or policies as needed. These en-larged functional cores of products can easily give you unwanted duplication of functionality and technology. Before you know it that can lead to fragmenta-tion of data as you wind up with multiple mailing lists within a single office or department. Some years ago, a task force was established in a large organiza-tion to look at the issues of data duplication and overlap. After research and conferences, it was determined that there were thirteen separate (and mostly

incompatible) customer files. When the task force presented what they considered to be an alarming report to management, the vice president responsible for systems said only that she was stunned that it was *only* thirteen.

Keeping in Touch with Web and Social Media

Today, most nonprofits have a presence on the web. Typically that presence is a website but more and more it is a presence on social media. as critical parts of the organization's communication strategy. The web and social media can provide you with powerful platforms to reach people and get the word out about your organization and the work you do. In addition to affording much broader reach at a significantly lower cost, they also function at a much faster pace than other communication tools (think printed flyers and brochures sent by mail). See Chapter 10, "Marketing, Communications, and Reputation" for more on the pros and cons, benefits and pitfalls of the web and social media.

What to Watch For

Web and social media resources and tools are phenomenally useful, but there are some risks to watch for. Here are some of the most common ones:
- Do not become distracted by social media tools and features (they are designed to attract attention after all). Stay focused on your organization's goals, message and reputation so that the content of communications is consistent regardless of platform or tool used. And, have a plan in place to monitor and respond in real time to comments and feedback.
- Remember that the web can be accessed from mobile devices. If you can't afford or just don't want to design for multiple platforms, the web and one mobile platform is quite reasonable. It also is easily expanded and mobile devices are in broad use.

Prevention

Remember that the demographic profile and audience demographics and use rates vary from platform to platform and reliance on mobile versus desktop devices vary and change a great deal. Using a social media platform to push out content to the general public or engage users and donors requires organizations to maintain an active presence on the web and on social media and monitor regularly consumer and workforce experience, feedback and ratings on public platforms. These new media and communications functions require staff and policies and processes to maintain and monitor them.

Among the risks in the social media world is going for numbers (looking to use platforms reaching the largest audience) regardless of whether it is the right audience for your message or conversely, limiting your use of social media to only those outlets that are popular among your staff and board.

Organizing Hardware, Networks, Devices, and Technology Skills

Technology has moved away from corporate mainframes to on-site servers, mobile devices, networks (wired and wireless), and a multitude of devices have come onto the scene. This proliferation of mobile and point-of-service technology has produced new risks for organizations, as well as helping them become more effective and efficient in their operations. One of the most significant issues in technology today is the rise of BYOD (bring your own device). This allows people to bring their own mobile devices to work and be productive. It may save money because some of the cost of providing technology to people is managed outside the organization. On the other hand, you need policies and guidelines to manage all of your technology assets including BYOD.

What to Watch For

As is the case with any organization, have a technology plan for acquisition and maintenance of hardware, software, maintenance, and skills across the organization in how to maintain, train and use them. New modes of communication ranging from cellphones to social media sites have become an integral part of modern life. Deciding on the best technology solutions for your organization can be overwhelming with all of the competing products and pricing options on the market. Some organizations convene a technology committee of staff, board and pro bono or paid advisors to help with scoping and purchase of technology.

Prevention

Nonprofit organizations have some specific issues to consider that government and commercial organizations don't have. Here are two of them:
- *Donations.* Nonprofit organizations may be recipients of donated hardware or mobile devices. Before accepting donations, make certain that it is functioning and has several years of useful life left. That is, it fills a gap in your technology

needs and aligns with your technology strategy. Having a "want" list for technology donations may be helpful to increase the likelihood that you'll get equipment you need. It will also provide a rationale for declining donations and limit requests for donation receipts for a tax deduction. The risk of being burdened with unusable or barely usable devices is not just the space they take up or the servicing that may be needed to use them. On top of that, such less-than-optimal devices may delay the needed acquisition of more useful equipment. Furthermore, make certain that donated equipment is sanitized so that it does not contain malware and that the donor's data has been removed. (Make certain that donors understand that removing their data is their responsibility.)

– *Grant funding of technology.* Funders look carefully at the use of their funds for technology acquisition. Make certain that you follow best practices in scoping, pricing and implementation of your acquisitions. Funders may expect a rationale for the valuation of in-kind donations of technology equipment when it is used as part of a match for a grant. Also, funders may sometimes have more information and perspective on the maintenance and support costs for equipment. Not to put too fine a point on the matter, make certain that you understand why the donor is giving the equipment away. In short, be certain that your technology acquisitions with grant funding adhere to the terms of the grant.

Developing and Acquiring Systems, Data, Apps, and Projects

Developing or acquiring technology solutions is an expensive proposition. Keeping up to date with updates and new versions for both hardware and software is a significant added cost that, for many executives and boards is surprising and out of reach financially. The argument that both the initial acquisition and subsequent changes are actually cost-saving in the long term is often true, but still hard to digest which makes budgeting, securing bids and developing detailed plans for implementation and annual use critically important.

What to Watch For

Major problems can occur with integrating systems. Among the most common risks are:

– Integrating systems without doing research and due diligence on what they can and will do for the organization is a risk to watch out for. It is easy to rely on marketing documentation rather than the fine print and details of application programming interfaces (API) but the organization's needs are likely to be addressed in the details of the APIs.

- Overvaluing the historical investment in existing (legacy) systems. It may have cost a great deal of money to implement a management system three years ago, but throwing it out today and replacing it with a different system might be a waste of money, or it may be an extremely prudent investment. As with cars, the value of investment in technology drops dramatically as soon as it is purchased and implemented.
- Ignoring or overvaluing the user aspects of systems. People grow to like (or loathe) the data systems and tools they use and they learn how to use them (or not). Avoid both extremes - balance human interest against organizational interests, recognizing that for many people, the hardware and software tools that they use turn into very personal matters.

Prevention

Preventing problems in acquiring, using and maintaining systems can be done with several basic practices. Pro bono guidance from expert volunteers and board members can be invaluable when their knowledge of the nonprofit's needs and organization practice combine well with their technical expertise. On the other hand, their participation in implementation activities can blur the lines between board oversight and management so this kind of volunteer work should be directed by an executive director with board oversight.

Most of these problems can be reduced to one point: Make certain you (or someone in your organization or a trusted consultant) understand the problems you're trying to solve, the technical details of the current solution, your in-house capacity to manage the technology platform, and the technical details of the proposed solution.

Particularly in organizations where in-house technical support is weak or nonexistent, remember that things will go wrong with technology—particularly in the development and acquisition of new systems. In these cases, make certain that you have backup and contingency plans.

Whether you hire consultants for the implementation of new systems, consider hiring a consultant to prepare contingency plans for the transition and switch-over. This expense should be budgeted and undertaken with the understanding that the best-case scenario will be to never need to use the contingency plans.

Summary

This chapter has highlighted some significant technology risk challenges in a broad manner. At this level of detail, board, management, and senior staff should be comfortable with the current and planned technologies for the organization and have clear expectations around what the technology can do and the kind of performance or management data it can generate.

We have addressed the various configurations of hardware and software—organization-wide standards and systems, as well as distributed standards and systems by functional areas. Today's world of technology is diverse and rapidly changing; any organization that uses technology has to decide how to manage change and innovation in technology. Are you a cutting-edge innovator in technology, or do you rely on proven technologies? For organizations that deal with the public, what technologies do you expect your clients, patrons, staff, and users to be comfortable with?

Chapter 13
Board Governance and Oversight

Boards of Directors or Trustees are responsible for providing guidance and oversight in nonprofit and commercial organizations. In the world of commercial organizations, the board also has a particular responsibility to protect investor interests as measured in profits. A nonprofit or NGO board also has the responsibility to protect assets, make prudent investments, approve an annual budget, secure an independent audit, and otherwise provide prudent financial oversight. But, they do it with a special twist, their responsibility is to maintain the organization's focus on mission.

The initial purpose for which a commercial organization has been created is likely to grow, change or lose meaning as time passes with little consequence so long as it is profitable. For nonprofit organizations, its mission is the ultimate expression of its value. All of the work a nonprofit does is either in the service of achieving its mission or a consequence of lost focus or mission drift. Much discussion of the role of nonprofit boards relates to risk centered on financial oversight and organizational sustainability. Yet, it is the unique role as mission-keeper that is key to a nonprofit's success.

Note: This is not to suggest that the mission of a long-standing nonprofit organization cannot change, but only to suggest that the constant objective for a commercial organization (which boils down to value) does not apply in the same way to nonprofits.

All boards have three basic responsibilities:
- *Duty of care.* Every board member has a legal responsibility to participate actively in making decisions on behalf of the organization and to exercise best judgment while doing so.
- *Duty of loyalty.* Every board member must put the interests of the organization before their personal and professional interests when acting on behalf of the organization or in any decision-making capacity.
- *Duty of obedience.* Every board member bears the legal responsibility of ensuring that the organization is in compliance with the applicable federal, state, and local laws and that it adheres to its mission.

There are other duties of board members and we will cover two of them as particular areas of risk:
- Creating a nonprofit or nongovernmental organization.
- Maintaining a sustainable board.

DOI 10.1515/9781501505942-013

Creating a Nonprofit or Nongovernmental Organization

Whether you are contemplating creating a new nonprofit organization or are dealing with an established one, it is important to understand the roles and responsibilities of its board. In addition to the responsibilities of nonprofit boards covered above, each organization delineates roles and duties in its articles of incorporation, bylaws, charters and other foundational documents that vary by jurisdiction. Bylaws and charters are subject to revision over time to meet new legal or regulatory mandates.

What to Watch For

In its simplest form, a nonprofit or nongovernmental organization starts with a person or group of people united by the desire to address a community issue or meet a community need. The issue that animates them can be as varied as providing health care, promoting the arts, protecting the environment and many other causes. At some point, this simple concept (a collection of people united by a cause) can evolve into a structured organization that can be organized formally as a corporation under the law.

Oversight of the new organization is provided by a board that provides oversight of operations and finances and offers guidance for other mission-related actions taken by the organization.

The first risk to watch for in governance and oversight is familiarity and consistent understanding by board members of the organization's mission and how the organization chooses to operationalize that mission. This is followed by how familiar each board member is with the rules, roles, responsibilities and accountability requirements that govern board and organization operations.

This is the most basic aspect of nonprofit risk, and it is listed here first because in organizations large and small, there often are misunderstandings regarding the scope of the organization's activities in support of its mission. Outsiders (members of the general public) as well as staff and board members will periodically ask, "Why can't we...?" Sometimes, the answer is simply that this is not part of the organization's mission no matter how worthy or critical the issue is. A focus on mission helps an organization make more informed decisions about all areas of operations—from programs and fundraising to technology and communications.

Founderitis (Founder Syndrome)

As the term suggests, this can be the initial founder(s)—often chief executives but commonly, one or more board members who have long been involved with or have held key leadership positions in the organization.

Founderitis is a term with a negative connotation although there are benefits to the experience that board leaders with a strong and long tenure with the organization bring that can be very useful. After all, with a powerful individual or group of board members, there may be a reduced burden on other members. Founding or longstanding board members can smooth the onboarding and transition of a new executive director and/or new board members. Founding board members can also be culture carriers and keepers of the organization's traditions. And, when it comes to fundraising, founding or longstanding board members may have a strong track record of cultivating and retaining donors.

The flip side of founderitis comes when tenure interferes with progress or needed changes in an organization. Term limits and executive contracts typically have end dates to prompt a review of performance and fit. When a board member or executive is unable to let go and they begin to hold the organization back from being able to meet its obligations or serve its mission, founderitis may be the cause.

All of these issues can be warning signs of trouble to come. If you look at media coverage of nonprofit organizations in the news, you will find many examples of these situations. Founderitis is notoriously difficult to handle because the founder is believed to have been responsible for everything the organization has accomplished to date. In many organizations, the founder has had a hand in everything from funding to plumbing and promotion of the organization. Boards are tasked with the challenge of helping a longstanding executive make a seamless exit. Executives are tasked with helping their board members and leadership know when it's time to move on and finding ways to acknowledge their contribution and commitment.

Prevention

Preventing governance risk extends to the relationships between the board, the executive director, the staff, and the public. Much writing has been done on the risk that comes when boards communicate and get all information from the chief executive only. Solutions offered typically include encouraging board communication with managers, staff and service recipients. This is a necessary but not sufficient protection from risk and it comes with some unique challenges for nonprofit organizations.

– *Board composition.* The composition of a board is outlined in the bylaws and other foundational documents of the organization. The number of board members, their terms of office, elections, attendance, and board committees are delineated in this way. The bylaws may include specification of types of members to be included such as representatives from the community, clients or service users. Nonprofit organizations with affiliates may require central approval of board members. Adherence to bylaws is the first step in risk prevention. If you do not adhere to these bylaws and other requirements, actions of the board may be null and void.

- *Open meetings.* Many nonprofit boards conduct their business in closed session with an open annual meeting once a year, while others welcome members of the public to any meetings. The organization's bylaws should define the organization's practice and notification requirements.
- *Term limits.* Best practice is to set term limits for board officers and members in bylaws. There are pros and cons to having term limits. One pro is that term limits allow organizations to bring in fresh perspectives and capacities. A con is that term limits that push out longtime board members can drain expertise and knowledge about the organization.
- *Meetings.* Nonprofit organizations must have at least one annual meeting where corporate elections and other routine business is conducted. Most nonprofits have quarterly board meetings as detailed in their bylaws. Organizations that do not hold regular board meetings should raise a red flag.
- *Attendance.* Bylaws typically specify a quorum that must be present or on a conference call to conduct business and vote or ratify decisions. This is often a majority of the board, but it is not always the case. Bylaws may also specify what "attendance" means. In some organizations, a board member who notifies someone (board president, executive director, or the like) is not counted as absent but as "excused." Board attendance is another risk for nonprofit organizations because of quorum requirements for voting and for decisions about continued board service for members who are frequently absent. Board minutes must include attendance. As noted previously, the absence of a quorum can make board actions invalid. Proper record-keeping is essential because some laws and bylaws specify that a certain number of absences automatically remove a board member. Comings and goings of board members during a meeting may alter the quorum. A roll call (or "quorum call") may be requested during the meeting to confirm the presence of a quorum at any given time.
- *Virtual attendance.* Bylaws or procedures may specify that board members can or cannot participate digitally. In some jurisdictions, laws governing nonprofit organizations may require in-person attendance.
- *Adopt and rely on meeting parliamentary procedures.* The manner in which board meetings are conducted, vary by country and type of organization; they may be specified in your organization's bylaws. It is important that there is consensus and formalized rules set to maintain order, move through the meeting agenda, take a vote. Bylaws should also cover how the organization will handle dissent and minority opinions. In the absence of agreement on the rules governing meetings, the board may be unable to act as a single body.
- *Keep minutes.* Board minutes must capture all organization decisions, activities and planned actions. These documents are often audited, reviewed by government or requested in discovery in litigation. Minutes are part of the organization's historical record and require care to produce and retain them. At a minimum, the

time and place of the meeting, attendees, agenda items and a list of all information and action items covered, major decisions and votes held during the meeting should be recorded.

Maintaining a Sustainable Board

The long term programmatic and financial health of a nonprofit organization means attention to board member expertise, commitment and networks. A strong board is animated by the organization's mission and its members are actively engaged in promoting it in a variety of ways.

What to Watch For

You can identify sustainability risks in three areas.
– Watch for communication, decision-making, attendance or contribution lapses by the board.
– Watch for role confusion, inappropriate communication, interference or conflicts of interest with the organization's priorities or policies.
– Watch for flagging interest, conflicts or lapses in adherence to board and organization policy by board members.

There are telltale signs of governance and sustainability problems on a board. Alone, each may not pose a risk to the organization. Taken together, they should flag attention.
– Absence of a quorum in board or board committee meetings.
– Absent a quorum, votes are taken and business is conducted anyway.
– Change in the number or frequency of non-present board members participating remotely.
– A change in member attendance patterns. This can be as benign as absence due to illness or personal matters (car repair that disrupts a carpool) or it can indicate communication problems, dwindling interest in the organization, personality conflicts or other underlying dysfunction.
– Board members who are unprepared for meetings because no material was provided beforehand or who hold key information that is not shared with other members (such as the treasurer, with responsibility for certain reports misses meetings).

Watch for role confusion with board members.

As part of a board's oversight, it observes and receives direct and indirect reports from the staff about the organization. Without micromanaging, strong boards monitor these reports, observe operations and regularly engage with staff as a way to assess what is actually happening within the organization. Role confusion, inappropriate communication or other dysfunction can spill over into organization's operations in unfortunate ways.

– Necessary operations are postponed because of board member absences or inaction.
– Board members find themselves in inappropriate situations.

Watch for problems with individual board members.

Board members are entitled to respect and privacy, as well as the recognition that comes from providing uncompensated and vitally necessary service to the organization. However, when circumstances prevent an individual board member from contributing fully or that impair their functioning, there may be cause for concern. Board relations and board relationship management is a critical function for a nonprofit organization. Organizations are confronted with delicate and highly sensitive issues in board management from handling personal information about board members and their families to changes in financial position or employment status and personality conflicts between board members.

Prevention

– *Board sustainability.* Over time, members of the board or other governing body often change. Keeping the board strong requires continuing work to recruit and retain members. It also requires serious work to manage board turnover, engagement and training, including attention to board members who cannot or whose capacities no longer match the organization's needs. Sometimes, long-time board members are reluctant to leave (and their fellow board members may be reluctant to suggest that course of action). A sustainable board addresses issue of recruitment, retention, engagement and training before those issues become crises. This is usually done in consultation with executive staff and the membership or nominating committee of the board.

  One strategy for helping board members move on while maintaining good relations is to create special categories of membership or affiliation. This can include establishing emeritus or honorary members who are recognized for their past contribution to the organization while not impacting the number of people needed for a quorum or other board actions.

- *Board member commitment.* Bylaws and Board recruitment activities must make clear what responsibilities a board member is expected to fulfill. Some boards are honorary, and attendance may not be required or expected. In such a case, make certain that at least some board members do attend on a regular basis.
- *Annual executive and board performance reviews.* The board is responsible for an annual performance and compensation review of the executive director and of the organization's operation. Strong boards also assess board activity and individual board member activity annually.
- *Interacting with staff and the public.* In general, board engagement in resolving disputes among staff or with clients is ill-advised.
- *Keep rules current.* Bylaws and other organizing documents should be reviewed on calendar so that they are up to date.
- *Clarify boundaries for board, staff, executive director, and the public.*
- *Weather disrupting meetings.* In climates where weather is a concern, many boards schedule multiple meetings—one for the normal meeting, and a prescheduled meeting in case the first one is rained/snowed/stormed out and canceled. One or two incidents may be coincidences or happenstance. Repeated weather disruptions that don't have planned alternate meeting dates constitute a risk.

Summary

Legally, the board is responsible for direction, financing and oversight—what happens in the organization. Jurisdictions differ in their requirements, but good resources for board requirements are a local charities bureau and web resources such as BoardSource (https://boardsource.org). A strong board is essential.

Many nonprofit organizations are able to recruit board members whose expertise they could not hope to obtain if they had to pay for it because people with such expertise share their skills with organizations that they support. In some cases, professionals are encouraged to share their skills with community groups as part of their responsibility to the public.

Organizations can reduce risk by identifying needed skills and capacities and recruiting for board members who have them. Depending on the organization, legal, financial, insurance, fundraising, communications, and client services expertise is most valuable. Other boards recruit individuals or community members who bring prominence, personal experience, legitimacy or access to the organization. Some boards have give/get requirements that require a certain level of financial contribution or fundraising. Each organization chooses its own route, and that may change over time as circumstances change.

Moving On

Whether you have decided to start your nonprofit risk project now, are still considering whether or not to begin one, are continuing with an existing project or are planning to use the strategies in this book to restart a dormant process, we wish you well and encourage you—more than anything else—to keep going. Every organization can benefit from a fresh look and there's much to be gained through an approach that takes nothing for granted.

Understanding and managing risk in your organization is not a sign of vulnerability or of a poorly-run organization. it is a sign of a responsible, forward-thinking leader and a future-facing nonprofit organization. We encourage you to come back to the tactics described in this book and to add new ones as you and your organization learn more about what works to keep your risks under control. We have additional information on our website at champlainarts.com/nprisk. We hope that one day soon, conversations about nonprofit risk become as ordinary and commonplace as discussions about nonprofit fundraising, board recruitment, and technology.

Index

* 9 7 8 1 5 0 1 5 1 5 1 6 3 *